MW01196231

Half a Saddle Off

Susan Carpenter Noble

Copyright © 2022 by Susan Carpenter Noble

All rights reserved.

No part of this book may be reproduced in any form or by any electronic or mechanical means, including information storage and retrieval systems, without permission in writing from the publisher.

This is a work of fiction. Names, characters, businesses, places, events, locales, and incidents are either the products of the author's imagination or used in a fictitious manner. Any resemblance to actual persons, living or dead, or actual events is purely coincidental.

Printed in the United States of America

First Printing June 2022

ISBN 978-1-956661-18-7 Paperback

Published by: Book Services
                www.BookServices.us

Contents

Dedications

Stacy Caidyn Beyale

When I first met Caidyn, I was struck by her deep love for her horse and her quiet determination to learn everything she could to improve her horsemanship. As we became better acquainted, I found myself intrigued by how firmly she had one foot planted in her father's Navajo culture, while simultaneously keeping her other foot in her mother's Anglo culture.

I got the idea that my book's main character, Meghan, would enjoy having a friend like Caidyn, a talented, smart, hard-working, and inspiring young woman. With guidance from Caidyn and her wonderful family, Autumn Rose and the rest of the fictional Ifaita family came into being. Special thanks to Caidyn's father, Irvin, for sharing his expertise with tips for coaching bull riders, and to her brother, Skye, for sharing the Navajo belief of how a horse can "roll away" one's anger and unhappiness.

Leila Thompson

This book is also dedicated to Leila, in honor of her love for her horses, including her mini, Speedbump, as well as her passion for all of her critters, whether they walk on four legs and are covered in fur (her horses, dogs, and cats), or on two legs and are covered in feathers (her chickens), or on eight legs (her adorable tarantulas), or even if they slither on no legs. She loves and cares for them all, continuously striving to learn.

Acknowledgments

Half a Saddle Off is a story about young girls changing into strong young women as they grow not just in knowledge by becoming better horsewomen, but also becoming stronger as they learn to deal with the sometimes chaotic emotions of being a young human.

In my own life, I've learned from and ridden with amazing, strong women, from my childhood 4-H leader Joan April Fry and fellow competitors/mentors Sis Doebler and Becky George in Pennsylvania; to Colorado horsewomen Carol Ackerman Dotta and Robin Funkhouser Cross; to Nevada QH breeders and All-around Horsewomen Laurie Shepard, Julie Lingenfelter, and Barbara Hodges; to International Three-Day Eventer Joren Traveller; to jockey, reiner, jumper, and artist Heather Larson. I am grateful to each of them for their friendship, teaching, and encouragement.

I am also grateful to my favorite children's librarian—my sister, Peggy Carpenter King—and to my daughter, Janet Noble. Thank you for your unfailing faith in my books and for spurring me on to improve the story lines.

Thank you to my editor, Betsy Hoyt, for her wordsmithing, faith, and encouragement, and to my publisher, Michael Feinberg, for his book design, layout, and creative covers. I am grateful to both for their belief that horse kids – and adults – deserve books about their equine interests.

Most important, thank you, dear reader, for coming along for the ride!

Half a Saddle Off

Chapter 1
A Moose and a Cat

"My horse is *not* an ugly moose! How could he say that! And how, Meghan Callahan, could you *ever* have thought anyone that rude was somebody you could like?" I asked myself out loud. Except I couldn't think of a good answer. I mean, Lane's good-looking, even though he's shorter than me, and he has a great smile, and he's a good roper, and he rides good quality horses, but none of that matters anymore. He has totally lost my respect. What an obnoxious thing to say to his sister's best friend!

Sadie and I have been friends since we found ourselves in some of the same eighth grade classes on my first day at her school in Fallon, Nevada, last September. We quickly learned we were both horse girls and, I don't know, we just sort of hit it off. We've been hanging out together for the past six months. Anyway, I *think* we're best friends. Unless maybe she thinks the same way her brother does and is secretly laughing at me behind my back.

1

I was so hurt and so angry at Lane that I wasn't thinking straight and couldn't seem to sort it all out. I grabbed my halter out of the barn and stomped over to my horse's pen. He immediately sensed I was upset about something and lifted his head way up high as I tried to put on his halter. That actually made me giggle, and I felt some of the anger draining away.

"Sorry, Freckles. You're not quite tall enough to get out of reach. Maybe you could've gotten away with that when I first got you, but I've grown. I'm finally catching up with you, big guy. In fact, I hope I don't outgrow you! Because I think you're perfect, no matter what *some* people might say."

I got the halter buckled and led him out of his pen and into the barn, where I tied him up so I could brush him. With his winter hair starting to fall out, I found a good use for my anger-induced energy and went to work, furiously rubbing the round rubber curry comb in big circles, pulling out huge clumps of reddish-brown hair. From the look on his face, Freckles was enjoying the process.

While I curried, my brain replayed the afternoon. My eighth-grade class had gone on a visit to the high school so we could tour the buildings where we would be attending classes next year. Lane had been out in the ag shop for his agricultural economics class when our group came through. He had announced loudly, "Hey, Meghan, I saw you riding one of those wussy saddles yesterday after school. I thought you were supposed to be a cowgirl. Why would you put some stupid little English saddle"—he'd said 'English saddle' with a total sneer in his voice—"on a big, ugly moose like your horse, anyway? You should be trying to cover up as much of him as you can."

His friends had all laughed. I had turned away, feeling my face turn red as waves of anger and humiliation washed over me. Just thinking about it was making me angry again, and I could feel my stomach tying up in knots. Riding English had not been my idea. In fact, I didn't like it at all, but Jeannie, my instructor, wasn't giving me a choice in the matter.

I curried harder, sending Freckles' loose hair and dirt flying in all directions.

A mournful sound stopped me.

I listened.

It was coming from the pile of horse blankets draped over the chair at the end of the barn aisleway. Looking over Freckles' back, I couldn't see who was making the noise.

I looked and listened awhile, before turning my attention back to my horse. Maybe I had imagined it. Even so, I was glad that, whatever "it" was, it had broken the anger loop that kept repeating in my brain. I took a deep breath and chose to think about something else, anything else, just as long as it wasn't Lane's comments.

I focused my thoughts on Freckles. It had been a year and a half since I sold my first horse—a little palomino mare I'd outgrown—and had been able to buy Freckles from the horse trainer in Colorado who taught me to ride. Ol' Ben had trained Freckles as a reining horse and a working cow horse. He'd then taught me how to do the fun reining stuff on Freckles: spins, sliding stops, rollbacks, and flying lead changes. I had ridden Freckles on cattle drives and trail rides. I had even taken him to a couple of horse shows.

Ben was starting to coach me on how to compete in working cowhorse classes when my dad came home with the bad news that we would be moving away. I got pretty hysterical at that because I thought I was going to have to leave Freckles behind. I mean, it was going to be bad enough saying goodbye to Ben and my friends Xender, Violet, and Emma, but leaving Freckles would have been more than I could handle.

Incredibly, Mom and Dad told me they were making plans to buy a horse trailer so we could take Freckles along too. Soon after, we moved to Fallon, Nevada, over eight hundred miles away.

We moved into a house outside of town, but it was still another mile to where I was keeping Freckles, so I usually rode my bike over. Sometimes I just rode the school bus all the way out to the ranch. That's what I had done today.

As I continued currying, I thought about how nice Freckles would look in a few more weeks when all my effort would be rewarded, and I'd be seeing the slick, burnished, red hair coat of summer. These spring days in northern Nevada were a lot warmer than what we had in Colorado.

Chapter 1 - A Moose and a Cat

There was that mournful cry again.

This time I saw a little yellow face peering out from among the blankets. When we made eye contact, it yowled even more plaintively, which I wouldn't have thought possible.

"Great," I thought, feeling more annoyance for the human race, "another abandoned cat for us to take care of." Fortunately, the lady who owned the ranch had a soft spot for animals, so this little one would undoubtedly have a home here. I wondered how long it would take before the new cat would allow us to touch him—or her. We'd had one last fall that was so traumatized by being dumped without the skills to fend for himself that he was totally skittish and shy. It took us months to earn his trust.

I continued currying Freckles, watching the big horse's head as he reached slightly in my direction, the white diamond-shaped snip on his nose twitching back and forth in pleasure as the itchy hair came loose off his body.

"You are such a goofball," I told him. "I know for a fact that you silly horses are firm believers in the idea 'You scratch my back; I'll scratch yours.' But you just keep that nose to yourself. You are not going to nip me again. I know. I know. You didn't mean to hurt me that time. You just wanted to tell me to curry harder. But getting my skin pinched between those giant chompers of yours really hurt. I had a black-and-blue mark for a week! So just you keep a respectful distance."

I was not making that mistake again. But I have to admit, it was kind of adorable watching him pretend that he was rubbing my back. I actually giggled.

Hanging out with horses is the best thing ever. The smell of the barn, that mix of hay, grain, leather, and horse, is my idea of aromatherapy. I was still currying hard, because Freckles was enjoying it, but I was having to work at it now that anger was no longer fueling my efforts.

The next cat yowl startled me because it was coming from underneath Freckles. Fortunately, he was used to barn cats and didn't even twitch as the stray rubbed up against his hind legs.

I was next. The skinny cat was soon focusing his attention on my high-top western boots, all the while continuing his mournful wail. The poor little guy (I could clearly see, below the base of his tail, that he was a guy) was painfully thin, with a ratty-looking, yellow tiger-striped coat.

"You sound so pathetic," I said, wanting to reach down to reassure him, but not willing to risk his claws or teeth. "Let's see if we can find you some food."

I carefully stepped away, barely avoiding his long tail while he continued trying to circle my feet and rub against my boots as I walked to the feed room where the horse grain and cat food were both kept. He shot through the door with me and leaped up onto a storage barrel as I reached for a spare bowl.

"Well, you were definitely a house cat, weren't you, Threepio?" (What else could you call a golden yellow

6

critter that doesn't shut up?) "I bet you were always jumping up on the kitchen counter next to your owner when a can of cat food was being opened."

Seeing his hope and desperation, I hurriedly scooped a handful of dry cat food into the bowl and carried it to the aisleway outside the feed room door. He plunged his face into the bowl the instant I set it down, going after the food as if he hadn't eaten in days. From the look of him, he probably hadn't.

Walking back toward Freckles, I aired some of my frustration. "How can someone raise a kitten and then just dump it when it gets past the cute-kitten stage? Some people are such jerks!"

I thought about that for a moment and wondered if it was contagious. Being a jerk, that is. There seemed to be plenty around.

I finished brushing Freckles, then picked up the hated English saddle out of the tack room and put it up onto Freckles' back, cinching it up just enough to keep it from slipping, but not tight enough to annoy him. Compared to the Western saddle I normally rode, it didn't weigh much.

After putting his bridle on, I realized what I'd almost forgotten. Pulling a hairband out of my pocket, I took a moment to run my fingers through my own hair, amused when I saw some of Freckles' red hair mixed in with my long, dark, wavy mop. I tied the mess back and jammed my riding helmet over it before leading Freckles out to the arena where I snugged the girth a little tighter and mounted up.

Jeannie wasn't just my instructor, she owned the place too, and she wouldn't allow any of her youth riding students, whether they were riding English *or* Western, to ride without a helmet.

"What took you so long? I thought maybe you had decided to body clip that hairy beast before coming out of the barn," Jeannie called from across the arena where she was schooling one of her training horses.

I wasn't sure if she was being funny or if she was annoyed. And after Lane's obnoxious remarks earlier, it bothered me to hear her refer to Freckles as a hairy beast, even though he was hairy.

In explanation, I simply responded, "You have a new cat."

"Somebody dumped another one?" she asked, trying to sound disgusted. But the reality was, she loved her barnful of cats and never truly seemed to mind getting more.

"A very mouthy yellow male." Tentatively, I added, "I named him Threepio."

"Perfect!" she laughed. The laughter definitely sounded genuine. "Well, we'll give Threepio a few weeks. If he has survived all the local coyotes by then, I'll take him to the vet for shots and tutoring."

She meant "neutering," I know, but she never wanted to say words like *that* in front of us kids. Personally, I thought that was funny, considering how many times I'd heard her cut loose with a string of cuss words when she'd hit her thumb with a hammer while fixing a fence or when a horse had stepped on her foot. Afterward, she would always apologize and tell whoever was in earshot that we shouldn't use that kind of language, and that it was a lot easier *not* to use it if you simply didn't start.

"Jeannie, do you really think Freckles can be a good show horse? Does he have the looks for it?" I asked.

"Of course he does, or at least he will when you get him shed out and shining again. He's never going to be Halter Champion. He doesn't have the conformation—the build—for that. But he's a nice enough looking horse. And he's a good mover with a good attitude. From my own point of view, I'd rather have a good-minded, athletic horse like him than a halter horse any day. I prefer riding them to just leading them."

That was reassuring anyway. Then I asked her something else, something I hoped would get me out of this uncomfortable mess. "Are you sure I can borrow this English saddle for the whole show season?"

"Of course you can use it. It's an older one, but it fits you and your horse okay. Just take good care of it; keep it cleaned and keep leather conditioner on it. That's all I ask." As an unnecessary afterthought, she added, "And don't you go buying a saddle without getting my approval first. There are too many details about getting a good, rideable English saddle that you don't know yet."

"Oh, I won't," I guaranteed her. That was a promise I had no intention of breaking. Ever.

"Darn it!" she shouted angrily, remembering to watch her language, "I told him not to come back here!" Tearing her gaze from the black Ford truck that was pulling into the long driveway, she glanced at me and said, "Start warming your horse up. This won't take long." She trotted toward the driveway, her long red hair tumbling loose as her sun visor fell off. No riding helmet for her.

Content to be alone with my horse, I walked him once in each direction around the dirt area that made up the arena, letting him look at the sights. There wasn't a fence around the arena. Jeannie didn't want her horses—or riders—dependent on a fence.

The enormous space was a little bit different each day, sometimes with trail obstacles, small jumps, or both, scattered around it; or on occasion, completely empty. Some women liked to rearrange furniture. Jeannie liked to rearrange arenas. "I want the horses to have a fresh look at things every day," she said. "I don't want them being bored, or, worse yet, complacent."

Only after Freckles had scoped it all out each day was I allowed to put him into a trot. We trotted around the arena, circling and reversing around the various obstacles, stretching Freckles' muscles—and mine—while getting him listening to my aids. "A warm-up isn't just physical," Jeannie was fond of saying. "It's mental, too, for both you and your horse. Use it to make sure you're tuned in to each other."

Chapter 1 - A Moose and a Cat

Freckles was definitely tuned in! He responded instantly to my aids: each small movement of my hands, any extra ounce of pressure from my legs, the slightest shift of my weight, and even the tone of my voice. The English saddle didn't seem to make a difference, as far as he was concerned. But it had been an adjustment for me. It seemed weird not having a saddle horn in front of me. And the shorter stirrups caused me to use some thigh muscles that, I discovered, weren't as fit as they needed to be. The insides of my knees were sore, too, where some of the skin had gotten rubbed off. When I complained about them, Jeannie referred to them as "fried knees" and said that if I rode in English riding breeches, that wouldn't happen. But since I didn't own any, I was just going to have to toughen them up.

After we had trotted for a while, I asked him to canter off on his right lead. He immediately rocked back on his hindquarters and pushed off into a canter that was only a *little* too enthusiastic. That's the one complaint my instructors always have about him. He's a seriously enthusiastic horse. His response to pretty much everything is done with too much power and too much bounce to the ounce. But personally, that's something I love about him. He makes me feel as if I'm sitting on a keg of dynamite ready to explode! But I know he won't. All that power inside of him is just waiting to do what I ask. We're a team, and that's an amazing feeling.

I think his attitude actually scares other people though, even good riders like Jeannie. She got on him one day to show me exactly how she wanted me to guide him through a difficult trail obstacle. But after only three steps, she got a funny look on her face, dismounted, and said, "Um, I think you should do this yourself while I explain it. You'll, um, you'll learn more that way." I ducked my head away from her while I nodded so she wouldn't see me giggling. And to be honest, I was glad she didn't want to ride him, because I don't actually want anyone on him except me.

I heard the Ford peel out of the driveway, throwing gravel up behind it, while Jeannie shouted words I couldn't quite make out, which was probably just as well or she would have felt obligated to apologize to me for her language again. Then she turned and long-trotted back to the arena on her mare. As she got close, she dismounted, picked up her visor, and put it back on her head to shade her eyes from the late afternoon Nevada sun. I saw her take a deep breath and turn off her angry ex-wife attitude in favor of her calm, in control, riding instructor face.

I found myself taking a deep breath and relaxing too, in relief.

"We should make a lot of progress over spring break," Jeannie started. "I really do think you can be in the running for the Youth All-Around Championship this year. That's my goal for you. You were thirteen the first of the year, right?"

"Yes. I won't be fourteen until June," I responded.

"Whatever. For the horse shows, your age on January first is all that counts. You'll be one of the younger riders in your age group. But I still think you have a chance. So, okay...when you go home today, you write that goal—Youth All-Around Champion—on a sticky note and put it on your mirror where you'll see it every day." She looked me in the eyes, her own blue eyes flashing with intensity, and said, "I mean that. I want you to focus on being a winner."

She waved me out toward the rail, the imaginary one, to start the lesson.

That evening, I wrote the sticky note as ordered, and I tried to think positively about being a winner, but Lane's mean words about Freckles had butted their way back into my head.

"I thought you were supposed to be a cowgirl. Why would you put a stupid little English saddle on a big, ugly moose like your horse anyway?"

His words seemed to be stuck in an endless feedback loop, keeping me awake and angry.

Finally, some coyotes started howling. It sounded like they were close by, although I could never really tell. I thought about poor little Threepio and hoped he was hanging out in the barn or the hayshed with Jeannie's other cats and staying safe. Thinking about the little cat interrupted the replays of Lane's mean words and I finally drifted off to sleep.

Half a Saddle Off

Chapter 2
Sore Legs

Most of Jeannie's other students were away during spring break. Sadie and her obnoxious brother, Lane, lived on the ranch next to Jeannie's, but they were gone for break too. I was okay with that.

On Jeannie's orders, I only rode English, trying to get better on my diagonals. I more or less understood the idea. I mean, I know that when horses jog or trot, they move their legs in diagonal pairs, with the right front and left hind hooves hitting the ground at the same time, then the left front and right hind hitting together.

Jeannie explained that the diagonal pair of legs is named for the front foot, so a left diagonal includes the left front and right hind. Apparently, it is totally important, when you're riding English, to be posting— going up and down in rhythm—in time with the left diagonal when you're traveling around the arena to the right, and vice versa when you're going around to the left. Jeannie made me practice that over and over.

Even though I wasn't in a lesson every day, Jeannie would still yell, either corrections or words of encouragement, when we were out in the arena at the same time, which was often. She had a lot of training horses to ride every day.

"Meghan, wrong diagonal! Look at his outside shoulder. You need to be rising up out of the saddle as that shoulder goes forward, then sitting lightly back down as it comes back under you. Your posting rhythm is very good. You're right in time with his trot. But you have got to be on the correct diagonal all the time. It helps your horse balance through the corners. Keep practicing!"

So I did.

I also got in a lot of extra hours of work every day: cleaning stalls, cleaning saddles, and cleaning the horse trailer. Jeannie had a lot of stuff on her spring-cleaning list. Of course, I also helped her rearrange the arena obstacles every day. But that was all good because I needed to earn some money for show clothes. I was hoping to get a new cowboy hat, a nice blouse, and maybe even a pair of show chaps. And I was also going to have to buy a pair of English breeches. I sighed.

At school Monday morning, I was anxious to see Sadie. It was a relief that she was acting like her usual self. It gave me hope that our friendship was still intact, regardless of how much I now hated her brother. But then, unless he had told her, she probably didn't know what he'd said because she had been in a different group than mine when I was going through the ag shop.

As always, Sadie was dressed in an expensive-looking blouse, tucked into her tight blue jeans. She wore a hand-tooled leather belt that sported an enormous silver buckle from one of her barrel racing wins. Her sparkling blue eyes and long blonde hair accentuated the dark tan she had gotten over spring break.

I suppose we look funny when we're hanging out together because she's about five feet tall, if she stretches up a little, and, the last time I was measured, I was five foot nine. Who knows how tall I am this week?

We both had the world's worst schedule, with P.E. class the first period of the day. After getting dressed and ready for school, who wants to start the day off by getting sweaty? It's gross. But at least it was a good time to talk.

"How was Hawaii?" I asked her.

"It was amazing," she gushed. "I learned how to paddleboard and went snorkeling and even took a couple of surfboarding lessons." Her face clouded briefly. "That's harder than it looks." Her megawatt smiled returned. "At least the instructor was really cute."

We talked, or at least Sadie talked, for most of the class. Since we were working on the weight machines, the teacher didn't mind the chatter, as long as we kept pumping iron. Finally, Sadie asked, "How was *your* spring break?"

"I rode and I shoveled manure," I told her.

"Wow. A regular joy overload," she laughed. Abruptly, her expression changed to serious, and she asked, "Is Jeannie calming down any?"

"Oh, she's still not fun like she used to be, but she's not freaking out as often. In fact, she only melted down once while you were gone, and that was after hanging up from a phone call. "I thought she'd go ballistic the one day, when her ex stopped by the ranch. And, well, I guess she did go ballistic on him, but when she came back to the arena, she was actually pretty cool. She told me she wants me to go for the year-end Youth All-Around Championship."

"She tried to talk me into that too, and I told her no possible way!" Sadie said.

"Why?" I asked. "What do you know that I don't?"

"I know that you're going to have to ride English if you're going to have a shot at the All-Around. That's why I won't do it."

"Yeah…" I wasn't sure how to answer.

"Anyway, I want to spend the summer focusing on my barrel racing and pole bending, and maybe even goat tying and breakaway roping. I plan to be on the high school rodeo team next year!"

"What about Deluxe?" I asked, picturing her gorgeous bay Quarter Horse gelding whose brown coat and black legs were slick and shiny even during the winter and spring. Sadie kept him blanketed during the cold weather to keep him from getting hairy the way Freckles did.

Chapter 2 - Sore Legs

"Oh, I'll keep showing him in Western Pleasure, Horsemanship, Trail—those kinds of classes." Her grin took on its ornery look, as it always did when she wanted to tease me. "So *you* will be riding for second place in them. But you can have that English stuff all to yourself."

The bell rang, cutting off our conversation before I could fire back, and I hurried to get to my algebra class.

After school, Sadie's first words to me when she rode Deluxe into the arena were, "Who is that ugly cat?"

"The scrawny yellow one?" I asked.

"Yeah. The one that yowls when you make eye contact."

"That's Threepio."

"Who?"

"Threepio. You know, the gold-colored robot from *Star Wars*, the one who talks a lot?"

"Never saw it."

"We watched some of the *Star Wars* movies for Dad's birthday a few months ago," I told her.

"I'm very happy for you," she said in a super-sarcastic voice.

"Anyway, someone dumped that poor little yellow cat and he found his way here," I said, continuing to trot around the arena, warming up.

"He wouldn't dare have stopped at our house. We've got five dogs now. And the Shepard ranch down the road must have eight. Jeannie's is the safest place for cats. That's why they all find their way here."

"Are all your dogs ones that got dumped?" I asked.

"No. We got two on purpose. But the other three were abandoned ones that we kept. Mom's a sucker for stray dogs. We'd probably have more, but if a dog shows up at our door, and my dad doesn't think it can be useful around the ranch, he hauls it to the pound and drops it off."

"Oh, that's sad. I've heard the pound here has a pretty high kill rate, 'cause they can't get very many of them adopted out," I lamented.

"Yeah. Well, we can't keep them all," Sadie said, with an air of practicality that belied the truth. It hurts to send an animal to its death.

⌒⌒

After we worked our horses in the arena, we headed out for a trail ride to cool them down. The irrigation canals that criss-crossed the valley were the perfect places to ride because they all had trails or two-track roads alongside.

"Oh, look! There's some wild asparagus!" I stepped down off Freckles to take a closer look. "That should be ready to pick in a few more days. Do you like asparagus?"

"Yuck, no," she said, watching me mount back up. "You are so lucky to have long enough legs to mount up like that, even on a horse as tall as he is."

"Well, it's not as if we get a choice on leg length."

"We need to do something about it," Sadie said.

"About what?" I asked, having no idea what her internal monologue was driving at, but feeling fairly certain she was no longer discussing asparagus or leg length.

"All the animals that people just throw away," she said. "It's not fair."

"No. It's not," I agreed.

We rode along in silence for a while, thinking about it. At least, I was thinking about it.

"Were you awake today when our class advisers were explaining we have to do a community service project?" I asked.

"Sort of." She looked puzzled. "Why?"

"Well, we could do some kind of a fundraiser to help with the problem," I said.

"What problem?" Sadie looked at me blankly.

"The stray animals!" I said impatiently.

"Oh," she said, then added, "So, how would money help them?"

"Well, I've been thinking about Threepio. I bet whoever dumped him did it because they found out how much it would cost to get him his shots and have him neutered. So they ditched him once he was past the cute kitten stage so they wouldn't have to put any money into him."

Still the blank look.

"We could raise money for a fund to help pay for that sort of stuff, especially for the neutering 'cause then there wouldn't be as many unwanted animals getting born."

Sadie brightened. "That's a great idea! We could maybe do a car wash!"

That didn't sound like any fun at all. Not that I minded washing cars. It's just that every time I'd seen a fundraising car wash, the girls had all been dressed in their bikinis, and, well, as tall and skinny as I am, I had no wish to go out in public in a bathing suit.

Out loud I said, "We can think about it and ask for ideas at our next class meeting."

⌒

My calf muscles and inner thighs were screaming at me even louder than Jeannie was.

"Stay up! Keep your backside from touching the saddle, but don't lean forward too far. You have to keep your legs directly under you while balancing your upper body. And don't slouch! Lift your ribcage up—that's better. Now, don't grip with your knees; you have to relax your knees and your ankles and just let your weight fall right down through your heels." Jeannie was barely pausing to draw a breath while she continued shouting corrections to my riding position.

Meanwhile, I was beginning to run out of breath. Trotting a horse had never been so hard. But then I'd never ridden a trot for fifteen minutes without being allowed to sit down. My barely-healed knees were starting to get the skin rubbed off again.

The only one who was relaxed about the whole thing was Freckles. He just kept trotting around the sixty-foot diameter round pen like he was enjoying himself, which he probably was. He liked to be moving.

"Okay, pick up your reins and reverse direction," Jeannie commanded. "But don't sit down! Stay up in two-point position. Then, as soon as he's going the other way, drop your reins and put your hands back on your hips. And keep standing, Meghan! You've got to develop a solid lower leg and good balance for your equitation classes and for when you start jumping."

"Okay," I said under my breath so Jeannie couldn't hear me, "but do I have to do it in just one lesson?"

Finally, she told me to sit back down and pick up my reins. "That's probably enough for now. But for the next few weeks, I want you in that English saddle every time you ride, even if you're just going for a trail ride. And I want you standing up in two-point, staying in balance, for at least ten minutes every time."

She opened the round pen gate and let us out.

I guided Freckles out to the trail along the canal, where we ambled along enjoying the spring evening. When we got to the spot where I'd seen the asparagus, I said, "Whoa," and Freckles stopped so quickly he nearly whip-lashed my neck. "Good boy," I told him, stroking his neck. "You've still got your reining-horse brakes, even when you're wearing the wrong saddle. You just hang onto that because we're going to have some fun in those reining classes this year. You can be a part-time English horse if that's what Jeannie insists on, but we're never gonna quit all the fun stuff like reining. We worked too hard on that at Ben's to give it up now."

I dismounted stiffly, pulled a bag out of my pocket, and bent down to snap off the asparagus. Once I'd gotten it all, I led Freckles toward another patch further along the canal. While I walked, or, more accurately, hobbled, along beside him, I scratched Freckles behind his ears the way he liked.

"Do you miss Colorado too?" I asked him. "The cattle drives and trail rides? I sure do. And I miss Ol' Ben. He taught us both so much! And I miss Xender. He was a good friend."

Arriving at the next patch, I picked some more asparagus and then managed to climb back up onto that saddle. My legs were so tired from all the two-point work that it was kind of a struggle.

Back in the saddle, I continued my musings. "It's funny, but I even miss Violet. Who'd have thought that was possible? But she turned out to be okay, once I got to know her. It's weird how you meet people and take a dislike to them. Then you get to know them, and when you find out why they are the way they are, you end up liking them. I guess it's that way with horses too. Except the first time I met you, I knew I liked you! You're the best horse ever, no matter what kind of saddle you're wearing! Lane is just an idiot."

At the end of the hayfield, we turned south and continued around the far end, coming back along the fence line between Jeannie's ranch and the ranch where Sadie and her family lived. As we got closer, I could see Sadie practicing the barrel pattern on Hobo. Hobo was a bay, like her show horse, Deluxe, but he wasn't quite as gorgeous as Deluxe. Even so, he had a slick, shiny coat from being blanketed all winter too.

Lane was riding his roping horse, a sorrel like Freckles. But where Freckles had a star on his forehead (not that you could ever see it through his long, thick forelock), a diamond-shaped snip on his nose, and one short, white sock on his left front leg, Lane's red horse had a wide white blaze down the middle of his face and four high white stockings on his legs. He was really flashy.

I watched Lane, who was focused on catching a plastic steer head that was attached to one end of a bale of straw. Once he'd caught it—he didn't miss very often—he'd shake his rope off it, coil it back up, and catch it again.

Lane was a sophomore in high school, and it seemed like most of the girls in school had a crush on him. I mean, he did have a great smile, and his brown eyes always looked as if he was amused by something. And maybe he was. Maybe he was always mocking other people in his head, if not out loud. I just had never realized it before.

As I rode closer, I noticed how Lane's dark hair curled out from under his cowboy hat. As usual, he was wearing a cowboy shirt, blue jeans, and one of his big silver belt buckles, which is pretty much how he was dressed in school every day. That's how all the guys—girls too—who were on the high school rodeo team dressed.

He made another catch, managed to shake it loose from the steer head, and was coiling his rope back up when he looked up and caught me watching him. He grinned and asked, "How could you ever rope in that stupid saddle? There's no saddle horn to dally to." Then he laughed at me and made another throw. This time he missed, which made me happier than it probably should have.

I didn't try to answer. His question didn't deserve an answer.

Sadie rode over toward me and I stopped on the other side of the fence. "I've got an idea for the animal shelter fundraiser," I said.

"We're not going to do the carwash?" she asked, disappointment in her voice.

"Yeah, we can still do the carwash, but I think we should do some other stuff along with it, like maybe a petting zoo, that will make money too."

"Well, that sounds okay."

"We'll talk about it at school tomorrow," I said. The sun was sinking rapidly and I knew she needed to finish working Hobo.

"Okay. Bye," she said as she turned her horse and went back to exercising him.

"Goodbye," I called after her.

"Bye," hollered Lane.

I turned my back and rode away without answering him.

Half a Saddle Off

Chapter 3
Cavaletti Poles and In-and-Outs

After our class meeting the following Monday, Sadie stretched up as tall as she could to give me a high five. "That was awesome! I can't believe how many of the kids want to help with our fundraiser! It makes me feel like one of the popular girls," she gushed.

That about caused me to get whiplash. "What do you mean? You *are* one of the popular girls."

She gave me an odd look before we went our separate ways to our respective classes.

Anyway, I was happy, too. We had decided to hold our carwash at the fairgrounds the weekend before the big 4-H and FFA Livestock Show and Sale in late April. But now it wasn't just a carwash! Several of the 4-H kids had promised to bring their project animals for the day and set up a petting zoo. There would be steers, pigs, lambs, goats, chickens, and rabbits. One girl, Sofia, said she'd bring her reptile collection, as long as she could set up in the shade of one of the big cottonwood trees. She didn't want her snakes to get too warm. She said some of her snakes were tame enough that she could wrap them around her arm, one at a time, and let people pet them.

A girl named Leila from my algebra class had volunteered to bring her miniature horse and offer cart rides. And a guy named August, whose mother worked at the animal shelter, had suggested we invite the shelter to bring dogs and cats for adoption that day. This was shaping up to be a lot of fun! And best of all, I wouldn't have to wear a bathing suit. I could help with the animal adoptions or the petting zoo instead.

After school that afternoon I warmed up Freckles, then listened while Jeannie explained the next step in my English riding torture. "One of the classes you'll be showing in is called hunter hack."

My brain immediately flashed on a knight in shining armor, hacking and slashing with his sword. Somehow, I didn't think that was the kind of hack it was going to be. Though that might have been fun.

Jeannie's voice brought me back. "Do you see those four poles, lying on the ground? Those are called ground poles."

"Well, duh," I wanted to say, but didn't.

Chapter 3 - Cavaletti Poles and In-and-Outs

"Or sometimes they're referred to as cavaletti poles, especially if they're raised a little bit above ground level. I've got the poles placed four feet apart, which should be about right for Freckles to trot through without hitting any of them.

"But before you trot, walk right down the middle of the cavaletti and tell me what you feel."

As I approached the poles, Jeannie yelled at me, "Look up. Those poles are his problem, not yours. You don't need to be looking down at them. Your job is to guide him over the center. So pick something in the distance and ride to it. Horses can feel it when you look down. When you're focusing on something on the ground in front of you, your horse will think you want to go *to* it, when what you really want, is to go over it and keep going."

We wobbled our way over the poles, not quite in a straight line.

"Come through again, but this time, the instant you come around the corner, pick out what you're riding to, so he knows where he's going. To *you*, it's a subtle difference. To your horse it makes a *lot* of difference."

As I started toward the ground poles, I focused my eyes on the upper branches of a cottonwood tree that stood way past the far end of the arena, right over the middle of the poles.

This time, Freckles went straight over them as asked.

"Much better," Jeannie said. "Now, what did you feel?"

"Well, we were definitely straighter, but it seemed like he hit almost every one of them with his feet," I answered, before asking a question of my own. "He doesn't hit them like that when we do the walk-overs in a trail class. Why is he doing it now?"

"Because they're set the wrong distance for walking. Remember? I said they're set for trotting. So try it." Her hands signaled me to go out on the imaginary rail. "Trot him about halfway around the arena, then make a big reverse and trot straight down over these, making sure to keep him exactly in the center. And keep your eyes up."

This time, he never touched a single pole. But I did notice a couple of other things. "His trot got really bouncy over the poles. And it seemed like he slowed down a little as he went through."

"Well of course his trot is bouncy. He has to pick his feet up higher than normal to clear the poles. But if he's slowing down, the poles are probably a little too close together. Let me lengthen the distance a few inches between each one and see if that helps."

She did, and I trotted him through again.

"That's perfect for him. Now let's work on you. Instead of posting through like you've been doing, I want you to stand up in two-point position and rest your hands halfway up his neck as you approach the first pole. Then stay standing until you're past the last pole," she said.

I nodded. How hard could that be?

But as I trotted through, Jeannie had to keep reminding me. "You're popping up on your toes. Keep your weight down through your heels so your heels are lower than your toes." And, "Keep your eyes up. Looking down throws your balance off, which adversely affects your horse. So don't start a bad habit like that." And then, "Get your hands further up his neck. I want them halfway up. If you need to take one hand off to guide him, do so, then put your hand back up there."

About the tenth time through, she said, "There! That looked good. Try it again and see if you can do it *right* more than once in a row."

And I did. In fact, I did it several more times until Jeannie was satisfied that I was honestly starting to get it.

A week later, after more days of trotting over the cavaletti poles, Jeannie placed a pair of jump holder-upper thingies a little over eight feet beyond the last ground pole. She stacked three more poles on the ground between the holder-uppers, one nested on top of the other two. Then she told me to trot Freckles through, keeping him straight and keeping my two-point position correct.

"But this time, I want you to grab hold of his mane halfway up the neck, not just rest your hands up there. And I mean grab a handful of it! It doesn't hurt him when you pull on his mane, so don't be shy about it!"

I wondered why, but this wasn't the time for questions, so I just did it.

Freckles trotted through the ground poles as usual, but then surprised me when he actually jumped over the tiny pile of poles.

Jeannie started laughing. "You never know what a horse is going to do the first time. Some hop over it like Freckles did. Some stop and then pop straight up like a piece of toast out of a toaster. Some land and start crow-hopping. They're all different—some horses are real drama queens—so you, as the rider, have to be prepared. By holding his mane, it keeps you from accidentally jerking him in the mouth when he does something unexpected."

Freckles was still trotting and, by now, we had gone nearly halfway around the arena.

"Come around and go through it again," Jeannie said.

This time he trotted through the whole thing, without hopping and without hitting anything.

"That's better," she said. "He didn't waste energy that time."

After a few more times, Jeannie made a little X by putting one end of each jump pole in the metal gizmos that stuck out of a hole toward the bottom of both 'standards,' which is what she called the things that were holding the jumps up. And apparently the metal things are called "jump cups."

We trotted toward the little X.

"Whatever you do, don't allow him to stop or go around the jump. He *has* to go straight through between the jump standards!" Jeannie told me. "Keep your heels down, your eyes up, and grab his mane!" she reminded me for the eighty-seventh time.

Freckles hopped over the little jump, just as he had the pile of poles. It was kinda cool! But the second time through, he just trotted over it again. Jeannie repeated that she was happy he wasn't wasting energy, but I thought it was more fun when he actually jumped it.

"That's enough for now," Jeannie said. "Give him a little rest, and we'll work more on your flying lead changes."

Over the next few weeks, Jeannie gradually raised the little jump until we were confident at the two-foot level. Jeannie kept warning me to make sure he didn't try to stop or go around the jump, because, she said, if he got away with that once, he'd always know that he *could* quit or "run out" if he decided to. Better, she insisted, never to let him find out that was an option.

She didn't need to worry so much. Freckles was clearly enjoying the jumping. He didn't show any interest in quitting.

"This time I've set up something a little different," Jeannie said as I rode into the arena one evening.

I wasn't sure why she thought that was news. It was different every day!

"This is called a one-stride in-and-out. These jumps are only about nineteen feet apart, which will give him room to jump the first one from a trot, land, take one stride, and jump the second one."

Before we could jump though, we did a long warm-up. Jeannie kept trying to help me improve my position, which was apparently an endless challenge. "Keep your hands steady. Don't let them go up and down with your body while you're posting. They have to be independent.

When I still wasn't keeping them steady enough, she said, "Stick your little pinky finger out and touch it against his neck. Now keep it there! Don't let it come off his neck. That will teach you how to keep your hands from moving."

Then it was: "Keep your elbows in."

I clamped my arms against my sides.

"Don't let your feet get out in front of you. We call that the 'toilet seat position' because that's what it looks like. So, unless that's the image you want to project, stand up in two-point and make sure your legs are underneath you where they're supposed to be. Then keep them there when you sit back down."

"Don't slouch like that! Lift your ribcage up; that will improve your posture."

She also had me work Freckles on staying consistent as we walked, trotted, and cantered around the arena the way we would do in a horse show.

Finally, she said, "Turn him down the center of the arena and trot through the in-and-out. He may take a cantering stride after he lands from the first jump. If he does, let him. As for you: stay up in two-point, holding his mane halfway up the neck from the time that you are one stride in front of the first jump until you're one stride past the last jump."

I turned Freckles toward the jumps as instructed, and his ears pricked forward in interest. He trotted to the first jump, landed at a trot, and trotted the second jump too.

"That was fine for his first time through. But you! Don't come up on your toes! Keep your weight down through your heels the whole way through. When you pop up like that, you're changing your balance, which messes with *his* balance and makes it harder for him to jump!"

We came through again, and Freckles put a cantering stride between the two fences, with what felt like a comfortable jump over the second.

"Nice!" Jeannie shouted. "He figured it out. And you actually kept your heels down. Come through again, and make sure you lift your ribcage. Don't go getting slouchy over the jumps."

We finally got several in a row where Jeannie was mostly happy with us. And, wow, it was fun!

At the end of the lesson, when Jeannie told me she wanted me to ride Western next time, I was almost disappointed, which kind of surprised me.

After I led Freckles back to the barn, talkative little Threepio greeted me from the aisleway.

"Well, meow yourself, little guy," I answered him. "You sure do sound a lot happier these days, even after your visit to the veterinarian."

As soon as I had Freckles' saddle put away and had curried all his itchy spots, I turned my full attention to Threepio. I almost had to. He hadn't stopped talking to me since I walked into the barn. He was sitting up on top of the pile of horse blankets, so I reached over and scooped him into my arms. His meowing stopped, instantly replaced by a loud purring that I could feel vibrating against my chest.

"I'm so proud of how quickly you've learned to stay out from under our feet when we're working around the horses. I know we all feel mean booting you away from us when we're grooming and saddling, but honest, Threepio, it's too dangerous for you, and for us too, to have you underfoot. Getting shoved away by our boots isn't going to hurt you near as badly as getting stomped on by a thousand-pound horse. Besides, you could trip one of us and then *we* might get stomped on. So, seriously, it was important for you to learn that."

He just kept purring.

"You sure are a happy little guy, considering it's only a week since your 'tutoring'," I giggled. "And you don't yowl any more. You just talk. And purr!"

He remained plastered up against me, staring into my eyes as I cradled him in my arms. "I'll never understand who could ditch a sweetheart like you."

⌒⟋

"The high school rodeo team is getting a mechanical bucking bull to practice on!" Sadie announced excitedly during P.E. class the next morning. "And..." she paused dramatically, "they're going to keep it at our ranch for practices!"

My pause was from confusion. "So...you're planning to learn to ride a mechanical bull?"

She looked puzzled. "Of course not! Why would I want to do that?" Then her smile was back as she said, "The guys will be coming out twice a week to practice at our place! Think of all that eye candy!"

"Ohhh..." Now I saw where she was coming from.

"They're going to use the lean-to on the side of our barn that faces the arena, which will help protect the bull from the weather, plus it's close to electricity to plug it in," she said, clearly proud to be in the know about the boys' plans. "And you'll be able to watch them too, from Jeannie's!"

"Um, thanks," I said.

"Well, I mean, you can come over too, anytime you want!" she assured me.

Our P.E. teacher yelled that it was time to go outside to continue our unit on softball, so I was spared having to come up with an answer that would hide my total lack of interest.

On Thursday after school, when it was time for my next lesson, I pulled my Western saddle out of the tack room, dusted it off, and, with effort, heaved it up onto Freckles' back. I'd kind of forgotten how heavy it was, compared to the English saddle. When I got his Western bridle out, I had to wipe dust off it too, especially the bit. Freckles didn't deserve to have a dirty bit put in his mouth.

When I mounted up, I settled into the saddle with a sigh of contentment, immediately reminded how comfy my saddle truly was. We made it to the arena before Jeannie showed up, so I started warming him up on my own. We worked first on the skills he needed for the Western Pleasure class. Freckles was impatient with the slower speeds. He was always happier with the English pleasure stuff, where he could stretch out his stride and cover some ground.

"Sorry, Mr. Enthusiasm, but you need to bring it down a couple of notches," I apologized, as we circled again to get him to slow down. By the time Jeannie showed up, he was giving me as reasonable a Western Pleasure jog as he seemed able.

"That's not bad, for him," Jeannie said. "And, wow, Meghan! You look fabulous! Your heels are down; your lower leg is solid; and I've never seen your posture looking better! All this English riding has really improved your position!"

"Sweet!" I said, surprised and pleased at the compliment.

"In your Western Horsemanship classes, most of the judges will probably have all of the riders do rail work—you know, just walk, jog, and lope both directions in the arena, and then they'll ask you to do a pattern of some sort," she said. "He looks like he's had enough rail work for today, so let's have you try a pattern."

"Sure," I agreed. The rail work wasn't my favorite thing either.

She told me a pattern to ride and, after a quick mental review, I started off. I urged Freckles into a walk toward the center cone, passing it on the right. But I didn't time my cues early enough and he didn't jog until we were past the cone, which wasn't good because she had said we should jog when my leg was even with it. The second cone came up too quickly and I was late with our lope too. We made a small circle, did a flying lead change, then circled, but bigger, the other way. When we got back to the cone, we changed leads and aimed for the far cone where we had a decent stop, but then I forgot to count the backing steps and was pretty sure I'd backed him up more than the five steps she had asked for.

"Well, your lead changes were nice," Jeannie said. "Other than that, you let the pattern get ahead of you, which really hurt your potential score. You need to be planning ahead. Take a minute to think about it, to visualize what you've been asked to do and *where* you need to be when you do it, then ride through it again. But this time, start your circles in the other direction, so he doesn't anticipate."

I walked Freckles back down to the starting point, then sat for a few minutes, planning. As I thought about it, this was nothing more than a simple, slow-motion reining pattern. Once I had a good picture in my head of where I needed to go and what I needed to do to make it happen, I looked over at Jeannie and nodded.

"Go ahead when you're ready," she said.

This time, I was prepared. I signaled Freckles earlier for each change of gait and managed to do them as my leg was next to each cone. Then I guided him through the loping circles so that they were the same size. And I remembered to count when we backed up.

"Much better," Jeannie said as we finished. "When you're riding on your own this week, whether Western or English, practice changing gaits at specific places. Don't just ask him to lope; ask him to lope when your knee is next to a particular clump of grass. Ask him to stop next to a particular obstacle. Got it?"

"Yes," I promised.

Except for the three orange cones, the arena was basically empty today. All of the jumps and trail obstacles were over toward one corner. It would be fun to do an actual reining pattern, with all that space available.

Jeannie must've read my mind. "Why don't you tune him up on his turn-arounds and then run through one of the reining patterns," she suggested.

"Yes!" I said eagerly.

Chapter 3 - Cavaletti Poles and In-and-Outs

I walked Freckles into the center of the arena and asked him for a soft, quiet, right-hand turn. He dropped his head, planted his right hind foot, and started pivoting around it. Slowly we built speed. I felt him step out of the turn with his hind feet and immediately bumped him with my outside leg. He stepped back under himself and continued the turn. After three more complete revolutions, I said, "Whoa," very softly and he stopped in place.

"He sorta leaked out on you for one step there, but you fixed it. Then he looked pretty good," Jeannie said. "How about the other side?"

I nodded and walked Freckles forward a few steps. Then I slid my neck rein a few inches up the right side of his neck and laid my right leg on him behind the cinch. Once again, his head dropped down, except this time he spun to the left. His speed built faster in this direction and he stayed correct on his hind end. After six complete revolutions, I stopped him.

"Wow," Jeannie said quietly. "That was nice."

I rubbed Freckles on the neck to let him know I thought so too.

Jeannie asked me if I remembered the pattern that started with four spins to the right, four to the left, and then into figure eights.

I did. After my mess-up on the horsemanship pattern, I took my time reviewing it with her and visualizing all the steps in my head. Then it was game on!

His left-hand spin was a little faster than his right, but not too different. His flying lead changes were dead center on his figure eights, and his slow circles were, well, not as slow as they should have been, but not bad. And his fast circles were flying! When we ran down for the rollbacks, one in each direction, he slid to a stop and turned 180 degrees to lope out in the other direction. Finally, we galloped down the arena for the sliding stop. When I said, "Whoa," I didn't even have to touch the reins. He tucked his hind legs up under himself and slid about twenty feet before coming to a complete stop. Then, with barely any pressure on the bit, he backed up so fast, it was a good thing I didn't have to count steps. I don't think I *could* have!

When I dropped my rein hand down onto his neck, he stopped backing and stood still, his breath coming fast. I laid forward on his neck, hugging him, and telling him what a good boy he was, while Jeannie, to my surprise, actually clapped her hands.

"That was amazing!" she said. "Now take him for a little trail ride to cool him out. He's earned it."

"Ben would be so proud of you," I told Freckles. "And of me too. He did such an amazing job of training you. And he was so patient with me, teaching me how to ask you to do your job."

Freckles walked along the canal, feeling totally relaxed. I wondered if he was still feeling the afterglow of that reining pattern as much as I was.

Chapter 3 - Cavaletti Poles and In-and-Outs

When we came around past Sadie's house, I was still lost in thought.

"Glad to see you came back to your senses."

I looked up to see Lane grinning at me. I walked on past without a second glance.

Half a Saddle Off

Chapter 4
The Fundraiser

The morning of our community service carwash/ pet adoption/petting zoo day finally arrived. I woke up to the usual, blue, sunny skies of the Great Basin Desert. Then after showering and putting on my best jeans, a lightweight, long-sleeved western shirt (to keep from sunburning,) and my new straw cowboy hat, I stopped for a quick look in the mirror. My hair was pulled back neatly in a ponytail (well, as neatly as it got.) My makeup looked good, thanks to Violet, who had taught me how when I still lived in Colorado. I kind of wished I had a fancy belt buckle for my plain leather belt. But nope. Maybe someday.

I turned for a sideways look. Hmm…That was disappointing. I had gotten in the habit of slumping. I guess I knew I was doing it, but all the other kids in my grade were so much shorter than me and I hated the feeling of towering over them. So I slouched to look shorter. Trouble is, it made me look really bad.

Jeannie's words popped into my head.

I lifted my ribcage.

The difference was amazing; I couldn't quite believe it. I actually looked pretty good. Wow.

Okay. This was weird. I was going into a situation where I was going to be around a lot of people. And I didn't have to feel totally awkward.

There was an air of panic at the fairground, as the few of us who had bothered to show up on time wondered aloud where the other helpers were, if any paying customers were even going to come, and, worse yet, would there be anything for them to do when they got here.

We divided up the signs that would show which way to go for the various events we had planned and spent the next ten minutes hanging them up. By the time we finished, trucks and trailers were arriving with the animals for the petting zoo. I showed them where to park and helped them find their pens.

By the time I finished, it was nearly 9:00 a.m., the official start time for our event. I was glad to see that everyone had shown up who was supposed to! Leila was there, harnessing her miniature horse to his cart. His name was Speedbump and he was adorable! As a bonus, Leila's mother was offering rides on a horse she had brought.

Chapter 4 - The Fundraiser

"I figured it was just as easy to haul two horses here as one. And since I had to be here anyway, I might as well have something to do for a cause as worthwhile as this," she said.

Sofia's reptiles were all snoozing in the early morning sun in their cages and aquariums. I noticed she had positioned them so they would be in the shade as the sun rose higher in the sky.

Three of the kids I knew from art class showed up unexpectedly and asked if they could do a face-painting booth. I pointed them in the direction of our class adviser, Ms. Klein. A few minutes later, I saw them setting up a small table and laying out their paints.

Meanwhile, August, his mother, and some other volunteers from the animal shelter made a large circle out of pet carriers so that visitors could walk around them and get a good look at all of the hapless occupants who were waiting for someone to love them. Next to them, one of the local feed stores had a booth to sell leashes, bowls, pet beds, and feed. That was a good idea. I wondered who had thought to invite them. Better still, they had a big sign that said 10% of all sales today would be given to the animal shelter!

Our carwash crew, armed with hoses, buckets, sponges, soap, and drying towels, were gathered at a large concrete area that sloped slightly down to drains. Sadie was with that group.

I consciously lifted myself straight and tall. Walking over to where they were filling their buckets, I said, "You look great, Sadie! Cute suit!"

She laughed. "It's funny to be here dressed like this. Usually when I'm slinging soap here, it's during the livestock show and I'm washing my steer. On those days there's green, slimy cow manure all over this concrete from all of the animals being bathed. And trust me, no one is here in swimsuits or flip-flops then. This is going to be a lot more fun!"

She didn't say anything about how I looked.

The first carwash customer pulled up, so I stepped back before I got soaked by the enthusiastic crew.

More cars were rolling in too. Those who hadn't come to get their vehicles washed were parking and getting out of the car, often with excited young children.

I hurried over to Leila and her mom, where my job was to collect the money for people who wanted to ride in the cart or on the horse. From where I was working, I could see kids filing through the petting zoo, reaching out to touch the critters while the 4-H kids shared stories about them.

Some people were stopping by Sofia's reptile display, fascinated to get to touch a snake, while others gave that area a wide berth.

My favorites were the kids who dragged their parents over to the pet adoption circle to find the dog or cat of their dreams.

Glancing to the side, I noticed a Native American girl standing about fifty feet away, watching intently as Leila drove her mini, Speedbump, around the field, the young passengers giggling in delight. Soon though, I was too busy to do anything but pay attention to the line of children queuing up for a chance to ride, either in the cart or on the horse. When I looked up again, the girl was gone.

The morning flew by, with more people coming out for our event than I ever imagined possible. At one point, someone from the newspaper stopped at our station and asked to get a picture of Leila and one of her little customers in her cart. The photographer asked me to stand next to Speedbump, "for perspective." So I stretched up to my full height.

Just after he snapped the picture, an old rancher, who was waiting in line with his granddaughter drawled, "That little horse sure is an efficient use of space!" Leila and I both burst out laughing.

By 3:00 p.m., the advertised end of our event, the crowd was starting to dwindle. I was surprised at how tired I felt. Keeping track of money and talking to total strangers all day was hard work.

As we gathered at Ms. Klein's car to turn in our proceeds, each of us counted our stack of money, then traded with the person next to us to count theirs. Then we traded with a third person. Once three different people had agreed on the amount of money in each stack, Ms. Klein took the money, put a rubber band around it, and added it to a large plastic bag. It looked impressive! When she read the final total, we all cheered and high-fived! She carried the money over to August's mother, who had just finished loading her empty crates into her truck. Only a few animals had not been adopted.

As Ms. Klein handed over the bag and told her how much was in it, August's mother looked a little stunned and a lot happy.

Ms. Klein continued, "The folks from the feed store will be sending you a check for the shelter's 10% share of their sales as soon as their accountant figures it all out. They said you should have it by the end of the week."

"I don't know what to say. I am so grateful! This is going to make a huge difference for the animal shelter."

Just then, the old rancher walked up, the one who had made me laugh earlier. He looked at the remaining dogs. "Well, shucks, he's still here."

I turned to look where he was looking, trying to figure out which dog he had his eye on. One old hound sat up in his crate at the man's approach, and I could hear the slow thump of a wagging tail.

"I promised that ol' fella that if he was still here by the end of the day, my granddaughter and I would take him home with us," he said. "I guess I better keep my promise."

August's mom barely managed to hold back her tears. "Oh, thank goodness," she said fervently. "This dog was scheduled to be euthanized this week if he didn't get adopted by Monday. Thank you!"

We all turned and left them to work out the details.

As we walked away, I saw several other people brushing happy tears from their faces too.

Chapter 4 - The Fundraiser

For a Monday morning, most of the kids in P.E. class were practically awake. Everyone was talking about our wildly successful community service project. I think they were all as surprised as I was at how many people showed up for it and how much money we earned for the shelter. One of the girls was super excited about the new kitten her parents had allowed her to adopt. Another girl was happy because the woman who owned the day spa in Fallon had talked to her at the petting zoo and had promised she would come to the 4-H livestock sale next weekend and bid on her market lamb.

I noticed that Sadie was uncharacteristically quiet. I finally asked if something was bothering her. In answer, she turned and pulled up the back of her gym shirt, showing me her sunburned back.

"Ouch," I said in sympathy.

"You're not kidding. It hurts," she lamented. "I managed to keep sunblock on most of the rest of me, but I guess I couldn't really reach my back or the backs of my legs very well. I'm really sore. And my parents weren't even slightly sympathetic. With the livestock show coming up, we had a lot of extra chores around home over the weekend, and they wouldn't let me off the hook for any of it."

"Ouch," I said again.

"Yeah. And Lane is being totally obnoxious about it. He slaps me on my back or flicks a rope at the backs of my legs every chance he gets."

"I thought your brother was Mr. Perfect," I said in surprise.

"He is," she said. "Usually. But sometimes he's a jerk."

It was all I could do not to agree with her. At least, not out loud.

⌣⟶

To my surprise, my after-school English lesson on Monday was just as much fun as my Western one on Thursday had been, but for totally different reasons.

Once again, Jeannie had set up two jumps right in a row, but these two were only about nine or ten feet apart.

"The last time he jumped, Freckles was able to put one full cantering stride in between the two jumps," she said. "This time, he will only have room to land and immediately take off. It's called a 'bounce' or a 'no-stride in-and-out'."

As we approached it the first time, she reminded me, "Eyes up, heels down, hands halfway up his neck, and grab mane."

For a change, I got it all together the first time through. And Freckles took it as if he'd done it all his life. We came through one more time, after which Jeannie added a third 'element,' as she called it, setting a third jump nine or ten feet beyond the second.

What a blast. I felt as if I were riding a giant kangaroo! Hop! Hop! Hop!

54

Chapter 4 - The Fundraiser

"You two are really looking good tonight," Jeannie told me when we finished. "Your position over the jumps is getting solid, and Freckles is snapping his knees up and looking very confident over the fences, no matter what I set up. Your rail work, too, is getting more consistent. He's a very nice mover. And his go-for-it attitude won't be held against him so much in the English classes." She hesitated. "I'm really proud of both of you." With that, she turned and walked back to the barn.

It was a gorgeous evening with plenty of daylight left, so I took Freckles out for a longer trail ride than usual. We continued west along the canal, going at least a half-mile past where we usually turned. Approaching the next crossroad, I heard a commotion and looked north toward the sound. A herd of cattle was streaming out of a pasture onto the road while a man on foot tried to turn them back. The cattle bolted past and took off fast enough to stay ahead of him.

I realized that if the herd got to the next crossroad and turned west onto it, they would soon be on the main highway. That could be catastrophic, as cars and trucks hurtled by at 65 miles per hour or more. Cattle —and people—could easily be killed if they collided.

In desperation, I pushed Freckles into a gallop, racing up the canal trail toward the road, trying to cut the herd off.

Freckles saw the cattle and turned on the speed. He knew this game and was quite happy to play. We charged out onto the dirt road and turned to face the herd. Freckles stopped and immediately went into cow horse mode, trying to turn them around.

I didn't have to do anything to help him, which was fortunate because my entire focus at the moment was in not falling off. I'd never ridden an English saddle while working cattle before. I sat back, dropped my weight down around him as he worked and somehow managed to stay with him.

The lead cow stopped and turned back, breaking the stampede. Pretty soon, the whole herd was turned and we followed them quietly down the road back toward their pasture. The man was out on the road, blocking it off and funneling the cattle back through the break in the fence where they had escaped.

Once we had pushed the last cow through the opening, Freckles turned and started for home. He knew his job was done.

The rancher, who had immediately gotten busy fixing his fence, turned and hollered, "Thank you! I appreciate your kindness!"

"You're welcome," I shouted back to him. "It was fun!"

"Well, I don't know about 'fun,' but I can tell you for sure, that was some fancy ridin' you did—especially if you take into consideration that you're about half a saddle off," he chuckled.

I turned away laughing and rode back the way we had come, happy to have been there at the right time; also happy not to have fallen off. As he had pointed out, English saddles are not ideal for that job.

Chapter 4 - The Fundraiser

Riding back past Sadie's place, I looked for her out in the arena, but only saw Lane there. I wondered what stupid remark Lane would make tonight. I didn't have to wait long to find out.

"When are you going to give up on that stupid wussy riding?"

"About the same time you give up being a jerk, which is to say, probably never." I was a little surprised when I realized what I'd just said, but the words just sort of came out. On the other hand, I was kind of pleased by his response. The usual grin was gone from his face and his mouth was hanging open in surprise. I don't think he was used to girls talking to him like that.

"Have a *wonderful* evening," I said sarcastically, with my best fake smile. As an afterthought, I added, "And try not to be quite so obnoxious to your sister. She doesn't deserve it."

If he responded, I didn't hear it. I rode on back to the barn, where I focused on taking good care of Freckles, including a thorough brushing, before turning him back out in his pen. Then I spent a few minutes cuddling Threepio.

"You're gaining weight, little guy. That's a nice round belly you've got going there." It occurred to me that not everyone would take that as a compliment, but in this case, that's definitely how it was intended. "You're looking so much better!" He was nestled into my arms, purring loudly and showing no signs of moving. However, I still had to get home for dinner, chores, and homework, so I finally had to peel him off of me.

Riding my bike home, I thought about the past few hours. The jumping had been an absolute blast! And accidentally getting to help with some cows was every bit as much fun! I should be feeling totally pumped. So why was I suddenly feeling down? Why did I feel hollow inside? It wasn't until late that night, when my brief conversation with Lane had replayed itself in my brain for the hundred and eighty-seventh time that I knew. It wasn't what Lane had said that bothered me. Well, I mean, it did, but that wasn't what was keeping me awake. *It was what I had said.*

Just because he was being a jerk didn't mean I had to be one also.

When the newspaper came out on Wednesday, Mom had it positioned on the kitchen counter so I'd see my picture from the fundraiser. It wasn't the picture the photographer had posed us for. Instead, it showed Leila and me laughing. It was really cute of Leila. But I was kind of bent forward. Mom thought it was great. Of course. That's what moms do. I think it's in their contract.

"It looks like you were having a terrific time, while doing something nice for the community. You should be proud of it, Meghan."

"Not so much," I said. "I'm all slouched over."

"You're laughing! It looks very, um, natural. It's a very nice picture and we're very proud of you." Definitely, her 'Mom contract' obligated her to say that.

Chapter 4 - The Fundraiser

"By the way," Dad said, "don't make any plans for this weekend. You were gone all last weekend, and every single one before that since we moved here. I know you like that horse, but how about spending some time with us for a change—a family weekend at home?"

"But the 4-H/FFA Livestock Show and Sale is this weekend!" I protested.

"Have I missed out on something?" Dad asked in mock seriousness. "Do you suddenly own a cow?"

"No, but all my friends will be there!"

"And your family will be here. And so will you," Dad said.

"You're going to be busy with your horse shows and working at the barn most of the summer," Mom said. "We'd like to have some of your time before you get even busier. Is that too much to ask?"

I sighed and looked down at my feet. "I guess not," I mumbled. There wasn't another answer that was going to be accepted.

On Thursday and Friday the school seemed almost empty because so many kids were gone for the 4-H/FFA show. On Friday, there were so few students in science class that our teacher asked if we wanted to go see part of the livestock show. Two kids didn't, so she let them go to the school library, while the rest of us walked to the fairgrounds. Since science class was right before lunch, I skipped lunch and stayed at the fairgrounds a little longer, which gave me time to walk around and see all of the washed and trimmed animals in their pens. I'd never seen such fluffy steers and sheep before. I even got to watch part of the Sheep Showmanship class and was surprised to see how the kids showed their sheep without so much as a halter or a rope to help control them. They did it all with their hands.

All of my friends were so busy with their animals, I didn't really get to talk to any of them, but at least I got to see what the livestock show was like and how much work went into it! As I was leaving, I unexpectedly came face-to-face with Lane. My stomach churned and I felt myself getting defensive and angry as I waited for whatever cutting remark he would make. He didn't say anything. He just walked by as if I didn't exist.

Good.

It turned out that my parents' idea of "home for the weekend as a family" actually meant helping install a sprinkler system, weeding the yard, helping with the garden, and doing some general clean-up. They gave me a few hours off in the afternoon to do homework, which I definitely needed for algebra and language arts. But at least the evenings were fun. Mom made barbecued chicken the first night, and Dad grilled steaks the second. Then we watched movies after dinner each night. I got to pick the movie the first night! The second night, Dad picked, so it was an action movie. It was okay, but I was so tired I fell asleep halfway through it.

Chapter 4 - The Fundraiser

Monday morning, I thought Sadie was going to fall asleep in the outfield during our P.E. softball game. She'd been late to class, and we hadn't gotten to talk before going out onto the field. But we did catch up for a few minutes when we went back into the locker room.

"What a weekend. I am so tired," she whimpered. "After the livestock auction Saturday afternoon, we helped with teardown, then drove four hours to the high school rodeo so Lane could compete in his events during the Sunday performance. He placed 4th in Calf Roping, but in Team Roping, his heeler missed so they didn't do any good; and he got bucked off in the Saddle Bronc event."

"How did you do at the livestock show?" I asked.

She managed a smile. "I had the Reserve Champion steer!" A split second later, she teared up. "I'm going to miss him. He was really fun to work with. He never tried to drag me around like some of my steers have."

"Does it ever get easier?" I asked, "Saying goodbye to an animal you've raised, I mean."

"Not really," she answered. "The only thing that gets any easier is taking care of them. I've learned *so* much about livestock care since I started." She began explaining her feeding program to me, and how she had learned how best to feed her steer so he would thrive, but the bell rang and we had to hurry off to our respective classes. I was sorry for the interruption. It had been fun seeing Sadie so serious about something she clearly cared about.

Half a Saddle Off

Chapter 5
Autumn Rose

After my weekend at home, I was super excited to get to the barn after school. I hadn't seen Freckles for three days! As I pulled up on my bike, Jeannie was on her way to the arena on one of her training horses. "Saddle up English today," she called back over her shoulder as she rode past me.

While I brushed Freckles, taking extra care to scratch all his itchy spots as a sort of apology, I told him, "I'm so sorry I couldn't spend time with you this weekend, big guy. But I know you had turn-out time, so at least you weren't locked in your pen all weekend. I'm glad for that. I hope—" I stopped talking, startled as someone unexpectedly rode past me. I hadn't realized there was anyone here other than Jeannie.

The stranger was riding a cute Paint mare. To my surprise, I recognized the rider. This was the Native American girl I had noticed at my class's fundraiser for the animal shelter. What was even more surprising to me was that she was riding English.

I closed my mouth, which, I realized, had been hanging open in surprise. Then I finished saddling Freckles and followed the girl out to the arena. She was already warming her horse up, so I started doing the same. Jeannie was loping circles on her training horse, ignoring us both. The other girl was focused on her horse, so I got busy warming up Freckles and myself.

Except for being aware of the other riders enough that I didn't run into anyone else or get in anyone's way, I tuned into Freckles and started our work. He was totally silly after his time off, so his stride was even bigger and bouncier than usual, which gave me some serious exercise as I worked to stay in rhythm with him, now sitting his trot, now posting. He was ultra-responsive anytime I asked for a faster gait but resisted noticeably if I asked him to slow down. In fact, the only times he slowed willingly were when I asked him for rollbacks. He would slide his hind legs up under himself, coming almost to a stop, before pivoting 180 degrees over his hindquarters and jumping out into a fast lope in the new direction.

I was having a lot of fun on him when Jeannie's voice broke in. "Meghan, would you try to remember you're warming up for an English riding lesson, not a reining class?" she shouted.

Chapter 5 - Autumn Rose

I got the hint and went back to working on making smooth transitions between the canter and the trot, all while keeping my lower legs in the correct position and maintaining good posture through my upper body. Fortunately, Freckles had gotten most of his playfulness out of his system with all of those fun rollbacks and eventually settled into the quiet work I was now asking him for.

After he gave me an especially nice downward transition from a canter to a trot, I stopped to let him rest and think. Jeannie and the new girl were both watching us.

Jeannie said, "Autumn Rose, please go out to the rail at a posting trot and show Meghan how to arc her horse correctly through the corners."

The new girl trotted out, apparently understanding what it meant to go out to the rail even though there wasn't a rail to go out to.

As she approached the imaginary far corner of the arena, Jeannie said, "Watch how she goes from having her horse perfectly straight as she goes up the long side of the arena, but then, as she starts into the turn, notice how she is bending her mare's body to follow the arc of the corner. Then as she finishes the corner, she straightens her out again. Now watch the next corner."

I watched.

After the girl had taken her horse both directions at a trot and a canter, arcing smoothly through every corner, Jeannie told me, "Now you get out there and try it."

As Freckles and I trotted, Jeannie shouted corrections. "You've got his head turned inside too much. You want his body *following* the curve, not exaggerating it." Then "Don't twist your body so much. Your horse needs to *feel* what you're asking for, but the judge shouldn't *see* it. Be more subtle." Finally, "Keep your eyes up. You don't have to tilt your head or look down. Just glance down over your cheekbones."

"Good, Autumn Rose," was all she ever seemed to say to the new girl.

Finally, when she decided Freckles and I were improving on our corners, Jeannie told us to stop and let our horses "air up" a little while she set up a few small jumps.

This time she asked me to go first. "Show Autumn Rose how to stand up in 'jump position' as you approach each fence, then stay up an extra couple of steps the way I had you do when you were first learning. I did as she said, and actually got a "Good, Meghan."

Then she told Autumn Rose to follow me through the jumps, and I heard her saying a lot of familiar things to her, things like, "Keep your weight down through your heels. Don't come up on your toes over the jump like that," and "Grab mane halfway up your mare's neck so you don't accidentally catch her in the mouth," and "Keep your eyes up."

Finally, Jeannie declared our horses had done enough and we should go for a cool-down ride.

We headed out of the arena and turned toward the canal, riding in silence for a while. Finally, I ventured, "By now you've probably figured out I'm Meghan, and

66

I'm pretty sure your name is Autumn Rose. Except I don't know if Rose is part of your first name or if it's your last name."

"My first name," she said quietly. "My last name is Ifaita."

When she didn't volunteer any more information, I decided it was up to me to keep the conversation going. "What's your mare's name? She's really pretty."

"Sage. And thank you."

"How old is she?" I asked.

"Eight."

Her answers were still very quiet. And they were getting shorter.

"Well, this is Freckles, and he's five."

"Yeah...I met Freckles when we moved in on Saturday. He's really sweet. Playful, too. I turned him out for Jeannie, and he bucked and played like a madman," she said.

"You moved in?" I probably sounded surprised.

"Do you see the big gooseneck trailer, up past Jeannie's house?"

I looked, and sure enough, there was a nice horse trailer—the kind that has living quarters in the front —parked near the detached garage off to the side of Jeannie's house.

Autumn Rose continued, without any prompting this time. "Dad agreed to work for Jeannie as her handyman in exchange for a place to park our trailer and keep my horse. So we'll be living here for a while."

"Great!" I said. "It will be fun having another English rider around. I was starting to feel lonesome."

Autumn Rose understood. "I get that. We're expected to ride Western in this part of the country."

While I was trying to figure out a politically correct way of saying what I was thinking, she said it for me.

"Especially me. Native Americans aren't expected to ride English. We're supposed to be cowgirls," she giggled, "and no one other than me seems to see the irony in that."

I burst out laughing.

"Other than you, that is," she said. "I could tell you were trying not to say it."

"Guilty, as charged," I admitted. "So how did you learn to ride English?"

"When we're not traveling, we live in northern New Mexico, near Farmington. I've been riding with a woman there who's an English rider, and she started teaching me."

"Sage really looks the part of an English horse. She's a beautiful mover," I said.

"Thanks. We worked hard to develop her movement. She used to have kind of a short, choppy stride, but my instructor made us do a lot of dressage work, and it really improved her gaits."

Chapter 5 - Autumn Rose

"Not to sound like a total dummy, but I actually *am* a cowgirl who only pretends to ride English, and I don't have a clue what 'dressage' is."

"It's a French word that basically just means 'training.' It's getting your horse cued in and listening to your aids—your hands, your legs, your weight—and developing some real teamwork. It's sort of like slow-motion reining," she concluded.

I laughed. "Now you're talking my language. Except in reining, there's one more aid: voice."

"Yeah, we use that too, but judges deduct points if they hear you," she said.

"You haven't jumped much though, huh?" I asked.

"Not really," she hesitated. "I've got a lot of work to do to catch up with you and Freckles."

"It won't take you long," I assured her. "You're a natural. It took me weeks to make the improvements you made in just today's lesson."

"Stupid way to ride a horse."

I looked up in surprise. I hadn't realized we had gotten to Lane's arena. He had already turned his back on us after his not-very-friendly greeting.

Autumn Rose shot me a puzzled look but didn't say anything until we got back to Jeannie's barn. "Is your neighbor always that friendly?" she asked.

"Only since I started riding English," I said.

Almost every evening after that, we went on a cool-down ride after we worked our horses. Lane mostly ignored us as we rode past. Sadie would at least wave.

As we headed out of the arena one evening, Freckles shook his head as if a bug had flown into his ear. I reached forward and gently used my fingers to rub his ear and chase the bug out. Once he was happy again, I relaxed back into the saddle.

"That's why I knew right away we were going to be friends," Autumn Rose said.

I cocked my head and looked at her, not sure I understood what she meant.

"I watched you brushing and talking to your horse before last Monday's lesson. I saw how you treated him—more like a friend than an animal. Then I watched the teamwork you two have. That told me what I needed to know about you."

I thought about that for a minute. Then I tried to say what I was thinking without sounding like a total dork. Finally, I just had to say it. "Wow! I'm honored."

"I'm glad. It was meant as an honor." After a moment's hesitation, she continued. "I don't care how people dress, or how they brag about what they can do. But I do care about how they treat their animals. If they're not good to their four-legged friends, well, they're not going to be fair or honest with their two-legged friends either."

Chapter 5 - Autumn Rose

We were approaching Sadie and Lane's place, where a small crowd was gathered at the side of the barn. The wannabe bull riders were practicing on the new mechanical bull. Autumn Rose held up her hand, signaling a stop, then put a finger to her mouth in the sign for "Quiet."

We sat in silence, watching the boys practice. One after another, we saw them getting dumped.

When one of them looked in our direction and pointed us out to the others, we walked on by and went back to Jeannie's, listening to jeers about our English saddles. Not that we cared. We were too busy trying not to laugh.

As we led our horses into the barn, we both lost it, laughing until our sides hurt.

"That was pathetic," Autumn Rose finally managed to say. "Those guys really need some decent help."

"Or some parachutes," I said. "Some of them caught a lot of air before they hit the ground."

"Have you ever ridden a mechanical bucking bull?" Autumn Rose asked.

"No," I admitted and stopped laughing. Ouch. Maybe I was being a jerk, making fun of them for something I'd never even tried.

"Me either," she admitted. "But I *have* ridden a bucking barrel. We used to have a 55-gallon barrel suspended between a couple of trees with ropes. My brother and I spent hours playing on it. One of us would climb up on the barrel, and the other would grab one of the ropes and start pulling it up and down and back and forth. You could make it a really wild ride!"

"That sounds like fun! Um...you have a brother?"

"Yeah. He's older than me. He's part of the reason we moved out here."

"How do you mean?" I asked.

"One of our uncles works at the mine out here and he told Ace—that's my brother—about a job opening. So after he graduated from high school last year, he came out and went to work. The job pays really well, which is what he wanted because he wants to save money to buy his own ranch back home."

"Isn't it free for you guys to live on the reservation? Why wouldn't he want to do that?" I asked.

"Why would he? He wants his *own* ranch, like we had growing up. He will probably buy something near Mom and Dad's place, which is near the res, but not on it. That way he can still be close to all of our extended family. Best of both worlds," she said.

"I've never lived near any of my extended family. Dad's work gets him transferred around a lot, which is bad because I miss old friends," I said, thinking about Ol' Ben, Xender, and Violet. Then I thought about Sadie and Autumn Rose. "But I guess it's good, too, because I meet new ones."

Autumn Rose smiled.

Chapter 6
Leave it by the Side of the Road

While we were brushing our horses the next evening, I asked Autumn Rose, "Have you met Sadie yet?

"Not officially. We've just waved."

"Well, she told me in school this morning that she's coming over for a lesson with Jeannie today, to work on trail obstacles," I said. "You two can finally meet."

"Oh, that must be what Dad meant this morning," Autumn Rose giggled.

"What do you mean?"

"When he came back to the trailer for lunch before leaving for his job at the hardware store, he said he had helped Jeannie build a playground for the horses this morning."

"Oh wow! No doubt Jeannie got pretty creative. This could be fun."

When I finished brushing Freckles, I went to the tack room for my Western saddle, while Autumn Rose saddled up English, as usual. We both mounted up and rode out to the arena for a look at the equine playground.

It was impressive. There was what looked like a deer hide draped across a jump standard right next to a mailbox. The wooden platform that Jeannie called a bridge sat over the top of a fat log.

I noticed that a notch had been cut in the bottom of the bridge to keep it positioned squarely on the pole. One end of the bridge sort of stuck up in the air a little. As a horse crossed it, the bridge was going to tilt from one direction to the other.

A bunch of pool noodles hung down from a wire, making a colorful curtain that we were probably going to have to walk the horses through. A blue tarp was spread out on the ground, the edges held down by tires. And a series of four cones was lined up far enough apart for us to weave around. Each cone had a colorful umbrella sticking up out of it.

"That's crazy!" I said.

"Yeah!" Autumn Rose agreed.

"We better get busy warming up our horses. If they're listening to us, it might increase the odds of our survival!"

"I can't argue with that," Autumn Rose agreed.

We finished our warm-up before Jeannie showed up and were letting our horses relax when a glowing vision appeared.

Chapter 6 - Leave it by the Side of the Road

"Hi Sadie! Did you get a new show saddle?" I asked.

She beamed, "My old one was getting a bit dated. This is what the big-name riders are using these days."

The amount of silver and bling on it was eye-popping. "That must be really heavy."

"Well yeah, it's heavier than my barrel racing saddle, but it's not too much more than my roping saddle," Sadie said. "So what do you think? Do you like it?"

While my brain scrambled for an acceptable answer, Autumn Rose chimed in with, "It's scintillating."

Sadie looked pleased, even though I don't think she knew what that meant any more than I did. I used the moment to change the subject.

"Sadie, have you met Autumn Rose?"

Before she could answer, Jeannie's voice boomed, "Are you girls going to have a gabfest or are you going to ride? Everybody get out on the rail and let's start with some equitation work. Then we'll try out the trail obstacles!"

Afterward, Sadie rode with us on our cool-down ride.

"I thought my horse was going to have a cow when the bridge tipped the first time," Sadie said.

"Yeah, when Deluxe jumped off of it sideways, I was afraid we were going to find out if your new saddle leaked," I teased her.

"I stayed on," she said. "And I still had *one* foot in a stirrup. That should count for something."

"Freckles wasn't too happy about those pool noodles over his head. It surprised me how scared he was at first."

"That's not his fault," Autumn Rose said. "A horse is a prey animal. He's wired to be afraid of strange things over his head. It could be a mountain lion preparing to jump down on his back, with all of its claws and fangs ready for the kill."

I shuddered at the picture she had just painted with her words. "I hadn't thought of it like that. Now I'm surprised he decided to trust me and go through it at all."

"That's what those obstacles are all about," said Autumn Rose. "Trust."

"Yeah, I guess so," I said. "I mean, it's not as if you'd ever see any of that on a real trail ride. Well, except for the deer hide and maybe the mailbox. But that other crazy stuff! If your horse trusts you enough to go through those, they'll probably go over or through anything you could possibly find in the natural world."

"I suppose so," said Sadie. "But ya know, I don't think I had nearly as much trouble getting Deluxe to walk over that blue tarp as I have getting him to cross real water. He hates walking in puddles. And don't even think about asking him to step into the canal."

"Well of course not," I said, pretending to be serious. "That tarp won't get his shiny coat muddy, but a mud puddle?"

"You're just jealous," she said. And the way she said it, I wasn't sure we were just kidding around anymore. I didn't know how to answer.

Fortunately, Autumn Rose redirected the conversation. "I was surprised how good they all were with the umbrellas. I was at a dressage show one time where the judge was sitting under an umbrella, and a lot of the horses were freaking out."

"Yeah, well those were all *English* horses. What else would you expect?" Sadie said pointedly.

Now it was my turn to change the subject. "Only two more weeks of eighth grade. I can't wait to be done!"

"Autumn Rose, why aren't *you* in school?" Sadie asked.

"I'm a home schooler," Autumn Rose said. "I should be finished with my studies by the middle of the week."

"Lucky!" I said. "What grade are you in?"

"Eighth. Same as you."

Out of curiosity, I asked, "How do you like it? Home schooling, I mean."

"It was great when I was little. Either Mom or Dad was home with me most of the day, and they always made learning fun. But since Mom went back to work full time, and Dad started working two jobs, I'm doing most of my classes online."

"Where do your parents work?" Sadie asked.

"Mom's a traveling nurse. She's on contract with the hospital here for the next few months. And Dad picked up a job at the hardware store, along with working here at Jeannie's."

"So if you're doing one of your online classes and you don't understand something, how do you figure it out when they're both at work? Who do you ask then?" I wondered.

"Well, some of my classes have actual teachers, so I can ask them when we're Zooming, or I can text them, or I can click on extra videos, or I can just wait for my parents to come home and ask them. But I'd rather get my work done during the day so we can just be together without having to do schoolwork when they're home. With the crazy hours they're working, we don't get to spend as much time together as we used to."

"Are you kidding?" Sadie asked. "That sounds wonderful, being home without your parents! My mom is always around and wanting to know what I'm doing. She never gives me any space. She even thinks she has to know who I talk to at school every day. And once I get home, she's always checking my phone or trying to listen to see who I'm chatting with. She is such a pain."

We rode along in silence for a few minutes.

Shouts and laughter got our attention as we approached Sadie's place.

"It must be later than I thought! The guys are practicing on the mechanical bull!" Sadie shouted "Bye" over her shoulder as she took off at a trot, hurrying for home.

Chapter 6 - Leave it by the Side of the Road

We both hollered, "Goodbye" to her retreating back.

Slowing our horses as we rode past Sadie's, we watched as the guys took turns trying, and mostly failing, to ride the bull. As the next cowboy got bucked off, the others laughed at him. He stood up, brushed the dirt and woodchips off his jeans, and tormented back, "Well, let's see *you* ride that thing!"

We watched two more boys try. Neither got it done.

"Entertaining as this is, I need to get home to study for my algebra test," I finally said.

"And I've still got a paper to write," Autumn Rose commiserated.

As we continued back to the barn, Autumn Rose said, "Those boys need help."

"No kidding," I agreed. "Rumor is they're trying to find a coach who actually knows what he's doing. But last I heard, they haven't found anyone. So they're just watching stuff online and trying to figure it out on their own."

"I'd hate to be trying to teach myself to jump without a real coach," Autumn Rose said.

"Yeah, that'd be a tough way to learn," I agreed. "I mean, watching someone online can show you what to do, but it can't tell you what you're doing wrong in real time the way Jeannie does."

"You let your weight come out of your heels over that last jump," Jeannie shouted during my next lesson. "Did you feel your lower leg swing back? Don't grip with your knees like that! Just let your weight drop down through your stirrups as if it's pouring out onto the ground! Try it again."

I circled around and came back over the jump. "Much better! Your lower leg stayed under you. That's where it's supposed to be, so it can be a solid foundation," she said. After I did it right a few more times she told me to rest my horse.

While she lowered the jump for Autumn Rose and Sage, she asked, "Do you understand what I mean by a 'solid foundation,' Meghan?"

"I think so…" I said hesitantly.

"Tell me," Jeannie commanded.

"Well, in church we learned that faith is supposed to be built on a firm foundation, like the man who built his house on a rock, not like the fool who built his house on the sand, so I guess a foundation is something solid to build on."

"Right," Jeannie said. "It's why they pack the dirt down firmly and then pour concrete before they start building houses. If the foundation isn't solid, the building won't stand for long. And if your lower leg isn't solid, you may not stay on top your horse when things go wrong. If he spooks or bucks or even trips, you may end up in the dirt."

"I spent enough time in the dirt with my last horse," I admitted. "I like it better up here."

Autumn Rose giggled.

"Your turn," Jeannie said. "Put Sage into a trot and take her over the middle of this jump, keeping your weight down through your heels the way Meghan did."

We watched as she came through; we could see the concentration on her face as she worked to keep her weight pushed down. I thought she did pretty well, but Jeannie found something else to correct. "Keep your eyes up! If you look down, that's just another way of inviting a wreck!" she yelled. "Come over here!"

Autumn Rose trotted over to where we stood, stopping next to us.

"Try to teach me, one step at a time, how to do a forward roll."

Autumn Rose looked as confused by the question as I was.

Jeannie repeated the question. "How do I do a forward roll? You know…a somersault from a standing position."

When neither of us said anything, Jeannie prompted us, "What should I do with my hands? Put them behind me? On my hips? In front of me? Where?"

"It seems like you'd want them out in front of you," Autumn Rose said hesitantly.

"Yes!" Jeannie said, extending both hands forward.

"What should I do at my hip?" Jeannie asked.

When neither of us answered quickly, she followed up with, "Should I lean backwards, forwards, sideways, or what?"

"Forwards," we answered in unison.

She bent forward. "Now, what about my knees?"

"You'll have to bend them," I said.

Jeannie bent her knees. "Okay. How about my head?"

"Well, you'll have to tuck it…kinda put your chin on your chest so you don't do a faceplant when you go into the somersault," I suggested.

"Yep," she said, tilting her head downward. "So, last thing: Where do I get the momentum to go into the forward roll?"

"Wouldn't you have to sort of push off with your feet?" Autumn Rose asked. "You know, kind of bounce up onto your toes and push off?"

Jeannie came up on her toes and looked, for a second as if she were going to launch herself into the somersault. But then she stopped her momentum and just sorta stepped ahead a few feet.

"From that position, I would've been able to do a forward roll." She laughed. "If I'd wanted to. But I'm not going to, because I have no wish to be washing sand out of my hair tonight. Though if we'd been on a grassy lawn or a rubber mat, I could certainly have gotten it done from that position."

We both nodded our heads in agreement, not understanding what this had to do with anything.

"Look at each other," Jeannie commanded. "Autumn Rose, where are Meghan's hands in relation to her body?"

"They're in front of her".

"Meghan, look at Autumn's hip joint."

I looked.

"Is it bent or straight?"

"Well, I guess it's sorta bent," I said.

"Exactly," Jeannie agreed. "Now how about the knees?"

"They're bent," Autumn Rose answered.

"Okay, so we're three for three so far. To do a forward roll, you told me to put my arms in front of me, bend at the hip, and bend at the knees. That's the same position you're in when you're on a horse." She gave us a few seconds to think about that and to wonder again what point she was trying to make. "So what were the last two things you told me, so I could do the somersault?"

"Tip your head forward," I said.

"And push up on your toes," Autumn finished.

"Perfect," Jeannie said.

"Oh! I get it," I said. "When you're on a horse, you don't want to look down or come up on your toes, because that puts you in the position to do a forward roll!"

"Yep!" Jeannie said. "And that's what riders do all the time. Think about it. When you've fallen off a horse, what direction have you usually gone?"

"Sideways," I said.

"Yeah, but I'll bet you didn't go straight sideways," Jeannie said. "Did you mostly come off in front of the girth or behind it?"

"In front of it, I guess."

"Me too," agreed Autumn Rose. "I usually seem to go over the horse's shoulder."

"No doubt you have," Jeannie said. "I'll bet I've gone off over the front end about 90% of the times I've gotten dumped. And from what I've seen, that's how it is for most riders. When we're on a horse, our hands pretty much have to be in front of us, and our hips and knees have to be bent. All we need to do then is let our weight come out of our heels and also look down for some reason. Then, if the horse gives us a little momentum by tripping, bucking, shying, or whatever, off we go, launched into a somersault, and we roll right off."

That actually made sense.

"So if you don't like falling off, keep your weight down through your heels and keep your eyes up," Jeannie said.

We both nodded.

"Now, Autumn Rose, go jump that again, with your eyes *up* and your heels *down!*"

Chapter 6 - Leave it by the Side of the Road

After the lesson ended, we rode out to cool the horses as usual.

"Seriously? You're not going to show in the Hunter Hack class next weekend?" I asked.

"I just don't feel as if I'm ready for that," Autumn Rose said.

"You're as ready for it as I am," I told her.

"No, I'm not. You and Freckles really have it together."

I laughed as I leaned forward to rub Freckles on his neck. "We've sure got her fooled," I told him, then looked up and winked at Autumn Rose.

"Besides, I don't have much money saved up for the entry fees; I want to use it for the classes I *really* want to enter," Autumn Rose added.

"I get that. I pay my horse show expenses too. It's nice to know someone else who does that. Sadie thought it was weird that my parents don't pay for everything," I said.

Autumn Rose looked puzzled. "Why should my parents pay for *my* hobbies?"

"Well, I pay for as much of it as I can by working for Jeannie," I hesitated, "though Mom and Dad help me out with some of the bills. They say my job is school, and they don't want me working a regular job."

"My parents want me focused on school too. And Dad shoes my horse for me, which saves me a lot of money, so I guess I'm not really paying for everything either," Autumn Rose admitted. "But they would never buy me a fancy show saddle like Sadie's parents bought for her. If I wanted something like that, I'd have to earn the money myself."

"Me too," I agreed. "But I'd never want to buy a saddle as flashy as the one she just got."

Autumn Rose got real quiet, so I turned and looked at her. She had a distracted look on her face, as if she might be giving some serious thought to something. As I was about to turn away, her expression changed, and she looked me right in the eye. "Why not?"

"Because I already have a Western saddle that I really, really like—one that I earned. It's just the right size for me, even with my long legs, and it rides well. Besides, I don't have to worry about cleaning all the bling. That's not jealousy, if that's what you're thinking," I said. "That's reality."

"I'm glad," Autumn Rose said.

Sometimes I didn't quite know what to say to her. So I didn't say anything.

As we rode past Sadie's place, Lane was practicing in the arena. He glanced up at us, smirked, and went back to his roping.

"Well, that was an improvement," I said, annoyed, as we rode out of earshot.

"What was?" Autumn Rose asked.

"All we got was a stupid look, instead of an obnoxious comment," I said.

She was quiet for a moment before finally asking, "Then why do you sound so angry?"

"Because he makes me mad. He knows it wasn't my idea to ride English. Jeannie is making me do this. Why does he have to be so nasty about it?"

Autumn Rose asked a question back. "Why do you care what he thinks?"

When I didn't answer right away, she went on. "You always *look* as if you and Freckles are having a lot of fun when you're jumping. And you've admitted that your Western equitation has improved since you've been riding English. So, are you really sorry that Jeannie is making you ride English?"

"Well, no. I mean, the jumping really is fun. But… well…" I stammered to a stop.

"Do you think I'm stupid for riding English?" Autumn Rose asked.

"No! Of course not! You and Sage are totally cool!"

"Then, Meghan, why isn't it okay for you to ride English?"

I had no answer. None that made sense anyway.

"You're upset right now, aren't you?" Autumn Rose asked.

"Not at you!" I blurted out. "I'm mad at Lane."

"How's that helping you?" she asked.

I hesitated, thinking about her question. Finally, I managed to mumble, "It's not. When I see him, my gut starts to feel all twisted up and yucky."

"You need to get rid of those feelings," she told me.

"How?" I demanded, not really expecting an answer at all and definitely not the one she gave me.

"Let your anger, your stress, and your yucky feelings flow out of you, down into Freckles' sweat."

"I don't want him to feel what I'm feeling!" I objected.

"Just trust me on this," Autumn Rose reassured me. "*He* will be fine. You just release all of your anger."

We were nearing the barn. I shut my eyes and tried to concentrate on letting go of the hurt and the anger I'd been carrying around inside of me, trying to see them slide down out of me.

When we finally dismounted, Autumn Rose told me, "Now unsaddle him and bring him over to the round pen."

I did as she said.

As we approached the round pen, she opened the gate. "Take him in, turn him loose, and watch what he does." As I unbuckled his halter, pulled it off his head, and stepped away, Autumn Rose continued, "He's going to lie down and roll. As he does, he's going to grind all of your troubles into the sand."

Freckles walked a few small circles, his head down, looking for the perfect spot. Once he found it, his front legs bent, he sank down onto his knees, lowered his hindquarters, and rolled over onto his side. He scraped his head and neck back and forth in the sand; then kicking with his hind legs, he rolled over onto his other side and rubbed that side of his neck. He rolled completely over again, and then once more. Finally, he straightened his front legs, rising halfway up almost into a sitting position. For a moment, he stayed like that, rocking forward and back as he rubbed his belly into the sand. Then, with a quick push from his powerful hindquarters, he was back on his feet.

"Keep watching," Autumn Rose told me.

Freckles gave his whole body a big shake, sending sand and loose hair flying.

"There went all of your troubles," Autumn Rose smiled. "Did you see how he shook them all off? And now that they're gone, your job is to make sure you don't pick them up again."

I actually laughed. I felt—I don't know—lighter somehow. But I wondered aloud, "How do I keep from doing that?"

"Easy," she said. "Just don't."

"But what do I do when he says something mean again, or gives me that smug, I'm-better-than-you look, like he did tonight?"

"Does getting angry when he does that help you in some way?"

I thought about it. "Well, no."

"Then choose not to care what he thinks. Meghan, it's totally your call. You have no control over what he thinks. You can't even know for sure *what* he thinks. The only thing you can control is how you react. So quit choosing to be upset. Don't pick your anger up again. Just leave it by the side of the road."

While I was getting ready for bed, I was still thinking about what Autumn Rose told me. I'd heard it before, that being angry with someone else just made your own insides hurt. And just a few weeks ago, my Sunday School teacher had talked about how forgiving others was usually a bigger help to you than to the person you were angry with. That hadn't made any sense to me when she said it. But after hearing what Autumn Rose said, I was beginning to think maybe it was true.

Chapter 7
The Sleepover

Sadie and I slammed our empty lockers shut and walked down the long hallway, escaping middle school and starting our first few minutes of summer break with high-fives. We walked toward her mother's truck and jumped in.

"Thanks for picking us up, Mrs. Hardin," I said as we buckled our seat belts. "It's great not having to ride the bus today!"

"Please, call me Angie. Calling me Mrs. Hardin makes me feel old." Sadie's mother laughed when she said it. "And you're welcome. I know you girls are anxious to get your horses ready for the show this weekend. I'm just sorry I won't get to be there to watch."

"It's just a horse show, Mom," Sadie said. "You and Dad need to go to Lane's rodeo. I get it."

Sadie sounded sincere, but the way she was sitting with her arms folded made her look kind of annoyed.

"It will be fun having Sadie stay with us for the weekend!" I said. "I haven't had a sleepover since I was in second grade."

"Really? Whyever not?" Mrs. Hardin—oops—Angie asked.

"Well, we moved to Colorado when I was starting third grade and my best friend there was a boy. For some reason, our families didn't think sleepovers were a good plan," I said, straight-faced.

Angie laughed again. Then she turned serious, "But I truly am sad to miss the horse show. I love watching my princess winning blue ribbons."

Sadie rolled her eyes.

Angie continued, "It will be so much nicer next school year when Sadie and Lane are both on the high school rodeo team. We won't have to split up anymore."

When I heard her say Lane's name, I felt my stomach start to tighten. Remembering what Autumn Rose had taught me, I mentally tossed my anger into a trash bag sitting along the edge of the road. I pictured all of my anger toward Lane being packed into that sack, and I made sure not to reach out to grab it as we drove by. I left my anger right there. I didn't even look back.

It felt good.

"Meghan?"

I think Sadie had just asked me a question.

Chapter 7 - The Sleepover

"Earth to Meghan," she said.

My eyes refocused on her. "Sorry," I said, "I was thinking about something Autumn Rose said."

"Oh yeah? What was that?" Sadie asked.

"She said I need to learn to focus on what's important."

"Yeah, well if she meant important things like conversations that you're currently a part of, you are doing a really bad job of following her advice," Sadie said.

"Sorry. What did I miss?"

"I just asked you when your parents are picking us up tonight, and do I need to haul my stuff over to Jeannie's or will they come over to my house?"

"I'm supposed to text them when we're done riding. Then they'll pick us up at your place."

"Well, that's very kind of them," Angie said. "The guys hope to have the trailer loaded and be on the road by 3:00, so it's nice to know I don't need to be worrying about my princess."

This time, I think I actually heard Sadie roll her eyes.

Once we arrived at Sadie's house, I thanked her mother for the lift again, then walked over to Jeannie's. Going past the Hardin's barn, I saw Lane loading his gear into their horse trailer.

"Good luck at the rodeo," I called cheerfully—and enjoyed the suspicious look I saw on his face.

When I arrived at Jeannie's barn, Autumn Rose was giving Sage a good scrubbing while Jeannie bathed one of her training horses. Jeannie saw me and called out, "You can take Freckles for a trail ride or lunge him in the round pen, but I don't want you doing arena work. If he's not trained by the night before a show, it's a little late to fix anything. So just go give him some exercise, but make it fun for him. Then get back here and bathe him and re-clip his bridle path and anything else that needs it."

I brushed Freckles, then swung up on him bareback and rode out Jeannie's driveway, across the road, and onto the canal trail in the opposite direction from which we usually went. It was a much longer loop going this way, too long for a cool-down ride following an after-school riding lesson. But now, finally, summer break was here!

I urged Freckles into a jog. Fresh as he was, he wanted to lengthen into an English trot, but I insisted he stay in a quiet jog so I could sit more comfortably. After about a quarter of a mile, I signaled him for a lope. For another half mile, we loped along in his smooth, rocking-horse canter. He was being such a good boy, holding his need for speed in check, but I could tell that if I encouraged him at all, we could be flying down the road at a gallop. Why not? I leaned forward and clucked. He responded instantly, turning up the speed as I bent low over his neck, exalting in his power as he raced along the road, his mane flying back in my face.

Chapter 7 - The Sleepover

Finally, I sat up and asked him to collect back into a quiet lope. He came back to me almost instantly, slowing his speed dramatically. I asked him to slow to a jog, which he did just as promptly. Finally, I told him to walk by settling my weight back slightly.

"You are such a good boy, Freckles," I said as I rubbed his neck. "And look at you, you're barely even sweating after that run, and you're not breathing hard at all. You're really getting fit!"

My voice was suddenly drowned out by an enormous roar that unexpectedly engulfed us from above. A jet was coming in for a landing on its way to the Fallon Naval Air Station, and we were directly under its flight path. I had heard jet engines before, but never this close! I could barely hear myself think as the roar rattled around and through me. It felt like I was inside a giant blender.

The noise finally subsided as the plane passed beyond us.

"Wow, Freckles! You handled that better than I did! You barely even flinched."

The deafening roar overwhelmed us again as a second plane came in over our heads. Freckles just walked along as if nothing unusual was happening.

Once the jet had passed, I put Freckles back into a lope for a little while to get us away from any more jets. We slowed to a walk long before we got back to Jeannie's, partly to make sure Freckles was properly cooled out, and partly because I knew Jeannie would lecture me if she saw me loping back toward the barn. I'd already heard her chew out one of her other students for doing that. She had told the woman that horses were inclined to be "barn sour" enough without the rider foolishly teaching them to run back to the barn.

Both Autumn Rose and Jeannie had finished bathing their horses by the time Freckles and I got back, which left the wash rack available for me. I traded Freckles' bridle for a halter, tied him, and picked up the hose. Freckles didn't seem to mind being hosed off, but even so, I started by spraying his front feet, before slowly aiming the spray higher and higher on his legs, eventually working it up to his chest, shoulders, barrel, and hindquarters.

Threepio wandered by, but decided that the water was splashing around too unpredictably for his comfort and quickly took himself elsewhere.

Freckles stood patiently as I washed him. Finally, as I was rinsing off the last of the soap, a flash of yellow caught my attention. I looked toward the movement and laughed when I saw Threepio balancing on top of the six-foot round pen fence. The little goofball took a few steps, lost his balance, and half-fell, half-jumped, down into the sand.

I turned back to Freckles and squeegeed water off him with a sweat-scraper, then wrapped my hands around his legs to squeegee water off them too.

All the other horses that needed baths had gotten them, so I left Freckles tied where he was to finish drying, while I filled the wash bucket halfway up with clean water and carried it into the tack room to clean saddles and bridles.

Chapter 7 - The Sleepover

Saddles. Plural. I was going to have to clean my own Western saddle as well as the English saddle that Jeannie was loaning me. Maybe, since I hadn't ridden my Western saddle much since its last cleaning, it wouldn't be too dirty. And there isn't nearly as much leather in an English saddle as there is in a Western, so that shouldn't be too bad.

Of course, I hadn't counted on Threepio's help. Threepio had apparently gotten tired of playing in the round pen and come back to the barn. As soon as I sat down to clean the first saddle, he was in my lap. That would have been okay if only he had just settled down and gone to sleep, but he immediately developed a fascination with my hair, batting at the curls. Fortunately, he did not have his claws out and was merely pawing at them.

Even so, he was making it awfully difficult to work.

I heard Autumn Rose laughing from somewhere behind me. I didn't try to turn around to look because at that particular moment, Threepio's front paws were resting on either side of my nose, and his face was about an inch away from mine.

"If you're planning to finish cleaning before dark, you might want to hang those saddles on the fence and stand up while you work," she suggested, still laughing.

"Good idea," I agreed, gently pushing Threepio off my lap and standing up. While I grabbed my Western saddle, Autumn Rose picked up the English saddle and the two bridles and followed me outside. We hung the saddles on the hitching rack, and I ran back into the barn for the bucket, sponge, and saddle soap.

Then I stood and cleaned my tack. Autumn Rose took pity on me and cleaned the bridles while I did the saddles.

"How did you get all of your stuff done so fast?" I asked.

"I didn't have to go to school for half a day like you did," she reminded me.

"Is that why you haven't been riding with me lately?" I asked.

"Yep. Since I finished school last week, I've been riding in the morning when it's cooler."

"I'm looking forward to that too," I said. "But I was bummed not to get to talk to you all week."

She looked at me questioningly.

"Remember telling me not to pick up my anger again?" I asked.

"Yes…" she said slowly.

"Well, it's working. At least, it is so far."

"I'm happy for you," she said, sounding like she meant it. "It makes life easier, doesn't it?"

"It does," I agreed. "So thank you."

Once my tack was clean and loaded into the horse trailer, I picked up the clippers and walked over to where Freckles was still tied up. He had dried off, so I was able to clip the bridle path just behind his ears.

Jeannie walked out of the barn with a lightweight horse blanket draped over her arm. "If you're all done, curry him off good, so he's not itchy and doesn't feel like he has to roll. Then put this sheet on him to help keep him clean overnight."

"Thanks!"

"No worries," she said. "It's one that I won a couple of years ago. It's too big for my horses, but it should be just right for him."

As soon as I got Freckles put back in his pen, I texted my folks to come pick us up, then walked over to Sadie's house.

Sadie was sitting on the front steps as I walked up, her overnight bag beside her, and her head down looking at her phone.

"Hi, Sadie."

She looked up, startled. "You scared me! I didn't even hear you coming!"

"Yeah, you looked pretty focused," I said. "Who is he?"

Sadie giggled, blushing. "One of the guys on the rodeo team."

"Which one?" I asked.

"Clay Corson."

I didn't know who that was, which she apparently realized from the blank look on my face.

"He's a rough stock rider: bareback broncs and bulls," she said.

"Oh, so he's one of the guys who's been coming here for practice."

"Yep. He's the guy with the curly red hair. He's sooooo cute," she gushed.

"I guess I haven't met him, though I think I saw him in the ag shop the day we went on the class visit." My stomach started its familiar twist. I consciously reminded myself not to pick up my anger from that day. It was hard. I took a deep breath, then breathed out the anger. On my next breath in, I thought about how lucky I am to have an amazing horse like Freckles. The twinge in my stomach started to ease.

I realized that Sadie had been rattling on about how wonderful Clay was and I hadn't heard a word. It was pretty much a sure thing that she would tell me all of his amazing characteristics many more times, so I wasn't too worried.

"Oh," she said abruptly, "here comes our ride. Don't you dare say anything about Clay in front of your parents! My mother doesn't know that he and I have been, um, talking, and I don't want her to find out."

"Okay."

The car stopped and Dad got out. "Hello, ladies," he said, reaching for Sadie's overnight bag. "Let me help you with that." He took it from her and put it into the back of our SUV. We all climbed in and started out Sadie's lane. Considering it wasn't a long drive home, Dad still managed to embarrass me. Twice.

"It's nice to meet one of our daughter's little friends."

He actually said that.

Sadie nearly choked, laughing.

"I didn't word that very well," Dad said.

Still laughing, Sadie replied, "Well, we're all 'little' compared to Meghan!"

I tried to laugh, but I think an eye-roll is all I actually accomplished.

"So your family is away at a rodeo this weekend?" he asked, in an obvious attempt to change the subject.

"Yep," Sadie said.

"We went to a rodeo the last place we lived, when Meghan was trying out for Rodeo Queen."

"Princess," I corrected him.

"Sure. Princess," he agreed. "Anyway, that was really wild, especially the bull riders. You'd have to be crazy to do that."

"That's one of my brother's events." Sadie wasn't laughing.

"What else does he compete in?" Dad asked.

"Saddle Bronc, Calf Roping, and Team Roping," she said.

We pulled into the driveway before Dad could go for number three.

During dinner, my parents tried to get Sadie to talk—about herself, her favorite food, her animals, or something—anything. Sadie mostly just gave one-word answers, while texting and scrolling on her cell-phone. After dinner, I helped clear the table and clean the kitchen while Sadie continued with her phone.

Since we'd gotten home from the barn late and were planning to get up early in the morning, we headed off to my room as soon as the clean-up was done.

I was looking forward to showing Sadie my model horse collection and my horse books and all the cool posters I had hung on my wall. But as soon as we walked through the door she said, "I'd like to get showered now, so I don't have to get up any earlier than I absolutely have to in the morning."

"I was thinking that too."

"Mind if I go first?" she asked. "I want to make sure my hair is completely dry before I go to bed."

"No problem. Mom put out a towel and washcloth for you to the left of the sink." I pointed toward the bathroom.

Without another word, Sadie grabbed her overnight bag and disappeared through the door.

An hour later, I gave up, reset my alarm for a half hour earlier, so I could shower in the morning instead, then fell asleep. Sadie must've got back from the bathroom sometime after that because I half woke up when I heard her giggling. I saw the glow of her phone before I rolled over and went back to sleep.

Chapter 8
Horse Show Morning

"I'm sure glad you don't have a lot of white on you like Sage does," I told Freckles as I curried off the manure stain he'd gotten on his butt overnight. Other than that one spot, Freckles just had some sawdust in his mane and tail from lying down. While I could get my horse clean with brushing and maybe a wet rag, Autumn Rose was frantically rewashing her mare's legs and part of one shoulder where the mare's white coat was covered in brownish-green stains.

"Are you ready for our big day, Freckles? I am. At least I think so. One good thing is that I'm not tired this morning like I thought I would be. My sleepover didn't exactly go like I imagined." I babbled away as I brushed him, a habit I'd gotten into when I lived in Colorado, where I'd worked around a lot of young or spoiled horses that my mentor, Ol' Ben, was retraining. He'd taught me to keep talking to them, especially when working around their hindquarters, so they'd always know where I was. That way I was less likely to startle them and get kicked.

"When I hear other girls' stories about sleepovers, they always talk about getting into trouble with their parents for staying up too late." I started picking the sawdust and the tangles out of his tail. "That's not how it was at all. Sadie was so distracted with her phone that she wasn't any fun." Freckles continued eating his hay. "Kinda like you, Freckles. You're so busy munching up your breakfast, you're not exactly giving me a lot of sympathy. Oh well, at least I'm not half-asleep this morning since I *wasn't* awake laughing and talking all night."

I finished his tail and started on his mane, which was hard because he kept moving to get to his food. Happily, it wasn't as tangled as his tail, and I was able to get him clean before Jeannie shouted, "Time to load up!"

As I led Freckles toward the trailer, I saw a splash of gold on top of the round pen fence. Threepio was going for a stroll along the top rail again. His route drew him even with the stud, one of Jeannie's training horses, who was standing next to the fence, half-asleep in the morning sun.

Apparently attracted by the expanse of gleaming, red horsehair beneath him, Threepio jumped down, landing neatly in the middle of the colt's back.

The stallion came to and groggily made a small hop to dislodge his unexpected burden. But Threepio clearly had no interest in losing his comfy perch. He popped out his traction devices and grabbed on more firmly.

Chapter 8 - Horse Show Morning

This time, I watched the stud react with an actual buck, tossing Threepio up into the air. He came back down onto the horse's back, claws fully extended, and dug into him with real determination. With that, the stud, now fully awake, went to bucking like he meant it. With each buck, Threepio got launched skyward, but every time, he was able to stick his landing. Finally, the enraged horse sunfished, managing to twist out from under him, and Threepio landed in the soft sand.

Threepio gave each of his paws a little shake and sauntered off, while the stud, who was apparently so angry he couldn't see straight, bit at him and struck at him with both front hooves, missing him repeatedly as he strolled across the round pen, under the gate, and back to the barn, perfectly undamaged.

We must have all been holding our breath because Jeannie, Autumn Rose, and I each exhaled a quiet 'whew' of relief, then started laughing that nervous laugh you do when a catastrophe is abruptly averted.

Jeannie was the first to snap back to reality. "It's a good thing cats have nine lives, 'cause there's nothing any of us could've done to save him." She loaded her training filly into the trailer, then asked, "Meghan, are you sure you have all of your tack, show clothes, hay bags, and buckets loaded into the tack room?" She nodded toward the open door that led into the front of her horse trailer.

"Yes, ma'am! I triple checked everything last night. Everything is in there except my cowboy hat and western show clothes. Mom has those in her car. She'll meet us at the fairgrounds by eight o'clock."

"Okay. Load Freckles into the trailer," Jeannie said, then turned and bellowed, "Autumn Rose, get your horse over here. It's time to load up!"

Autumn Rose untied Sage from the wash rack, where she had finished toweling her off, and led her over to the trailer too. Once the horses were all in the trailer and we were shutting the door behind them, I said to Autumn Rose, "Looks like you got all her extra spots off.'"

"I love Paint horses," Autumn Rose replied. I laughed because she sounded as if she was trying to convince herself.

As we finished latching the trailer door, Jeannie asked us again, "Are you sure you have everything?"

"Oh," I said and ran over to grab the bag I had set down by the barn door when Mom dropped me off earlier. "Now I do."

We climbed into the truck with Jeannie and headed for the fairgrounds.

"Um, don't we have to pick up Sadie and her horse?" I asked, confused.

"Sadie texted that she's not done with her chores yet and doesn't want to go to the fairgrounds until after the English classes," Jeannie said. "And since I plan to come back to get the other training horse later, it's not a problem."

"Oh. Yeah, I guess it takes awhile since she's having to do everything herself," Autumn Rose acknowledged.

Chapter 8 - Horse Show Morning

In my head, I silently added, "Especially since she has to get it all done in between texts to her boyfriend."

"You *will* do something with your hair before you go into the show ring, Meghan?" Jeannie made it sound like a question.

"Yeah, it was still wet when I left the house this morning. I've got a brush and bands with me to tame it down," I promised.

"Good," Jeannie said, then added, "By the way, your makeup looks really nice."

"Thanks!"

"Autumn Rose, you look nice, too, but please tell me you're planning to put your hair up under your helmet," Jeannie said.

"No," she said hesitantly. "It makes my helmet too tight and gives me a headache."

"Well, I guess the braid will work for today. It will stay neat and won't be too distracting. But next time you buy a new helmet, get one big enough to tuck your hair under. In English classes you're expected to have your hair neatly out of sight. Braids on English riders are only okay if you're under twelve years old," Jeannie said.

Autumn Rose looked down, mumbling, "Oh."

I could see an abrupt change in Autumn Rose. The excitement in her eyes was gone and she seemed almost to wilt like a plant that hadn't been watered.

As we pulled into the fairgrounds, Jeannie said, "After we unload the horses, I'll go to the show secretary's stand to pick up our numbers while you two start getting ready."

I hatched a scheme, and as soon as Jeannie was out of sight, I ordered, "Put down that horse brush and come over here!" Autumn Rose looked up from where she had been despondently brushing her already gleaming horse. She walked toward where I had set up a folding chair.

"Meghan's Hair Salon?" she asked, sounding hopeful.

"If it's okay to change your beautiful braid, then yes."

She sat in the chair. "Make it happen!"

I reached for the long, single braid, undoing the band at the bottom. Then I quickly unbraided it, brushed it out, and got busy doing a French braid that started at the hairline above her forehead. I continued the braid down the full length of her hair, then wound it into a tight bun, pinned it, and put a hairnet over the whole thing. I handed her the helmet, and she put it on.

"How does it feel?" I asked.

"Perfect!" she said, taking the hand-held mirror I offered and walking to the truck's outside rearview mirror, where she looked at it admiringly. "Will Jeannie approve?"

"We'll know soon," I nodded in Jeannie's direction. She was walking back toward us.

Chapter 8 - Horse Show Morning

I took the hairbrush and started frantically brushing out my own hair in preparation for braiding it too.

"Well, that's a big improvement. I like it!" Jeannie said, circling around Autumn Rose. Then she looked up at me. "You need to quit dawdling and get your hair done, Meghan. The arena is open for schooling."

Autumn Rose looked as if she was about to jump to my defense, but I smiled and promised, "I'll hurry."

While I braided my own hair and got it pinned up on my head with hairnet and helmet firmly in place, Autumn Rose brushed the travel dust off both Sage and Freckles. We saddled up and were mounted before Jeannie had her young training horse ready.

"Do you want us to wait for you?" I asked, managing not to giggle.

"Yeah," Jeannie said, ignoring the real intent of my remark as she slipped the filly's bridle onto her head and buckled the throatlatch. "This is her first show. She'll take courage seeing how your horses accept all the noise and the sights."

She mounted up and we all rode to the arena.

I walked Freckles all the way around the outside edge of the arena, first one direction, then the other, allowing him to look everything over. Occasionally, I would drift into the center and do a couple of curls in each direction to make sure he was being attentive to my reins.

Once he was sure of his surroundings, I eased him out into a posting trot to loosen up his muscles and my own. We did some big circles at a trot, once again checking that he was soft to the reins while simultaneously stretching his muscles laterally side to side. I asked him to collect his trot, slowing his speed but keeping his energy up. As he responded, I could feel his back come up and saw his neck arch slightly downward as he rounded his whole spine. I thought for a minute before the word came to me. Jeannie called this longitudinal flexing.

Then I extended his trot, keeping his backbone rounded as he lengthened his stride down the straight-away.

After we did those same exercises the other way, I asked him to canter first one direction around the arena, then the other. When I asked him to come back to a walk, I simply stopped my body's cantering rhythm and settled down deep into the saddle. He promptly responded, without sliding to a stop as he would have done if I had picked up the reins and said, "Whoa." Jeannie had really worked us on that skill, explaining that doing sliding stops was frowned on in English classes.

I walked him to the center of the arena, stopped, and just watched the other horses for a few minutes. It was kind of a madhouse, with riders working their horses in different directions at different gaits, but somehow, it all worked out.

Chapter 8 - Horse Show Morning

Autumn Rose trotted by, working on Sage's collection. "Nice!" I called out to her as she went slowly past.

I noticed that Jeannie's horse was finally trotting calmly past the bucking chutes that lined one side of the arena. The filly had been pretty terrified of the chutes when she had first come through the gate, but Jeannie had somehow gotten her over it. Now she was trotting past with confidence.

Jeannie managed to canter the filly around each direction before the announcer came on the microphone to advise everyone that it was time to clear the arena so they could start the show.

Jeannie's horse was right under one of the speakers when the announcer spoke and the filly, startled, jumped sideways from the unfamiliar noise. Jeannie sat up there as if she were glued to the saddle and was able to bend the young horse's nose around into an exaggerated curl until she started to relax.

Just then, the announcer called for the exhibitors in the Leadline class to start gathering at the in-gate. The filly was clearly startled again, but didn't react quite so dramatically this time. Jeannie stroked her neck in approval. The announcer spoke again, saying something about coffee and hot chocolate being available at the food stand, and the filly didn't even flinch. Once again, Jeannie leaned forward and stroked her neck. She then dismounted and led the filly out of the arena.

Autumn Rose and I dismounted also, leading our horses to the gate and back to the trailer. We offered each horse a drink of water, put on our hunt coats (onto which we had pinned the lightweight, cardboard numbers that would identify us to the judge,) wiped the dust off our boots, and rode back toward the arena.

From the announcer, we learned that there had been a four-way tie for first place in the Leadline class. Three of the four children were led out of the arena, each wearing a big smile and holding a blue ribbon. The fourth tiny exhibitor was clinging to the saddle for dear life and crying that he wanted off the horse! His embarrassed mother held his blue ribbon and the horse's reins in one hand and his belt in the other, trying to keep him from falling off as he wriggled and screamed.

"I don't think this is going to be his favorite sport," Jeannie observed.

I couldn't argue with that.

Autumn Rose and I stopped far enough from the gate to be out of the way while the adult riders trotted their horses into the arena for the English Pleasure class. Jeannie waited for the other exhibitors to go in first, then urged her filly through the gate, following them.

"She looks as if she's holding it together pretty well," Autumn Rose said as Jeannie's filly trotted past the bucking chutes.

"Yeah, she does. She's a pretty mover too," I said, mentally comparing her to the other seven horses in the class.

"Look at that chestnut mare with the flaxen mane and tail," Autumn Rose said. "What's she doing?"

I had noticed the pretty red mare with her almost-golden mane and tail too. And since I had seen this kind of horse before, I actually knew the answer. "She's a gaited horse; maybe a Tennessee Walker. They don't trot. Instead, they do something called a 'running walk.' A trainer near where I used to live had them. They're really smooth to ride when they do that."

"Wow! They're fast too," Autumn Rose said as the gaited horse began passing some of the other horses.

Just then, the little boy from the Leadline class ran up into the grandstand, causing a surprising amount of noise as his little, booted feet pounded up the metal stairs toward the man waiting for him.

Unfortunately, Jeannie's horse was just trotting past as the strange sound echoed off the grandstand roof and down into the arena. The filly leaped sideways, away from the racket. Jeannie calmly put her into a circle and trotted back around. She circled one more time and the filly settled back into a steady trot.

"Jeannie sure doesn't shake loose," I said. "She's amazing."

"She *is* amazing," Autumn Rose agreed.

A low whistle got my attention, and I turned to see my parents walking toward us.

"Look at you in that fancy suit coat," Dad said. "You look nice."

"It's called a hunt coat, Dad," I told him, feeling the blush rising in my cheeks. Dad had a real talent for embarrassing me. Even so, it was nice hearing I looked good.

"And look at that gorgeous posture," Mom added.

My face got redder.

"Um, we're just about to go in for our first class. You can probably see best from the grandstand." I pointed toward it, hoping to hurry them on their way. As they walked off, I added, "Just try to walk quietly so you don't scare the horses."

They got to the grandstand just as Jeannie and her young horse were cantering past. Their first steps on it were pretty noisy, and Jeannie's filly jumped just a tiny bit, but then they walked more softly, and Jeannie got past without any more excitement.

When the placings were called, Jeannie placed sixth out of the seven riders. One lady's horse had had its head so far up in the air that I'm not sure how she could even see around it. On top of that, she had then taken the wrong lead one direction at the canter. The judge had obviously decided that even Jeannie's inexperienced horse looked like more fun to ride than that one.

Jeannie was all smiles, stroking the young mare on her neck as they walked out with their green sixth place ribbon. "That was a good experience for her," she said as she rode past us. Over her shoulder she called back to us, "Don't forget to enter the arena at a trot. And get your heels down."

The announcer was calling our class into the arena, so we both stood up in our stirrups to make sure our heels and lower legs were in position and then trotted our horses through the gate. There were twelve riders altogether, so I immediately focused my efforts on getting Freckles out of the crowd. Once we were by ourselves, I relaxed a little. But I still kept my heels down.

The announcer called for a walk. I stopped posting, settled into the saddle while stretching my upper body even taller, and Freckles dropped back into a walk. The next command was to canter, so I dropped my outside leg back and moved his hip slightly toward the center of the arena; then I pushed with my seat and he stepped off into the correct lead. I was careful to keep most of my weight in my legs, which would help keep my legs directly under me. I remembered Jeannie's comment that if my legs got out in front of me, I would look as if I were sitting on a toilet instead of on a strong, beautiful horse!

After we cantered, the announcer called for a walk, then a reverse. I made a big, wide reverse to the inside, trying to give the horses that were now in front of us time to get even farther ahead. I wasn't about to let Freckles get into the middle of that crowd. That's a lesson I learned the hard way at my very first horse show. I had allowed the little mare I was showing to get boxed in, and when the horse ahead of us broke gait, it had forced my horse to do the same.

With Freckles' big stride and ground-covering walk, he was catching up to the others, so I started looking for a way to put more distance between them and us. Fortunately, the announcer called for a trot again, so I allowed Freckles to continue walking for a few extra steps while the other horses trotted off. Then I noticed they were all cutting the corners of the arena, so I guided Freckles deep into the corners, which put us further behind them. I was a little surprised when the announcer called for a canter instead of having us walk first, but I knew it wouldn't be a problem. I collected Freckles and stepped him out onto the correct lead.

Finally, the announcer said, "Trot in and line up."

I brought Freckles back to a trot, then stayed out on the rail long enough to figure out where there was space for us. The other riders were pretty close together, so I trotted to the end of the line-up, leaving lots of room between the last horse and Freckles before I stopped.

The judge walked down the line, asking each of us to back our horses. Then she marked her score sheet with her decisions and handed the piece of paper to her young ring steward. The girl ran over to where a clipboard dangled from a long string that came down from the announcer's booth, which was built above the bucking chutes. She clipped the paper to the clipboard, and it was pulled up like someone would reel in a fish.

The microphone clicked on, and the winner was announced: number 243. I looked down the line-up to see who stepped forward. It was Autumn Rose and

Chapter 8 - Horse Show Morning

Sage! I whooped in delight and started clapping. I almost didn't hear the second place number called, and even then I wasn't sure. But when I heard my parents joyfully screaming my name, I realized it was Freckles' number. We stepped forward too and rode toward the gate to pick up our red ribbon.

Jeannie was positively beaming. "Well done, ladies!"

Once we had gotten far enough from the gate that we weren't in the way of the twelve-and-under riders entering the arena, I dismounted, practically into my parents' arms. They were hugging me and petting Freckles and jabbering about how proud they were.

When I could finally get a word in, I said, "Mom, Dad, I want you to meet my friend Autumn Rose."

Autumn Rose smiled shyly. "I'm pleased to meet you, Mr. and Mrs. Callahan."

"Congratulations on winning that class!" Mom said.

"The people sitting just down from us sure were excited when the results were announced," Dad said.

"That would probably be my parents," she said. "They're the two people wearing cowboy hats, about four rows up from the rail."

"They're smart. That morning sun is shining straight into the stands. It'll be nice later in the afternoon when it's shaded, but it's brutal this morning," Dad said. He turned toward me. "What do you think? How would your dear ol' dad look in a cowboy hat?"

"Good. But only if you let me help pick it out!" I said, already imagining what a dorky-looking hat Dad would choose if left on his own.

"Ah, a date with my favorite daughter!" Dad said.

"Um, we need to be getting ready for our next class," I hinted.

"Oh, of course, sweetie," Mom said. "We'll go back up to the stands."

"And squint into the sun," Dad added.

"Just try to suffer in silence, dear," Mom told him.

As they walked away, Autumn Rose grinned at me. "They're pretty funny."

I just shook my head.

The kids in the arena were being called into the center to line up. Then the announcer said, "Let's bring the next class in on the rail, while we're waiting for the results."

I looked around and saw Jeannie, who was trotting her filly around a small warm-up area. She stopped her, backed her up a couple of steps, then turned toward the arena. Clearly she was trying to keep the filly's attention on her between classes.

In a sudden panic, I turned to Autumn Rose. "Do we have a pattern we have to learn for the English Equitation class?"

"No. There's no pattern for Equitation this time. I asked Jeannie about that earlier. She said the judge might call for some different stuff or might tell us a pattern we have to do after we're already in the arena, but there's nothing to memorize beforehand."

"Oh, good," I sighed in relief.

We watched as Jeannie trotted past us, through the gate, and almost all the way around the arena, stopping near the bucking chutes. She got there just in time to watch the ring steward attach the class results to the clipboard on the string. As the clipboard started upwards, Jeannie's young horse stared at it in wide-eyed wonder, raising her head to watch until it disappeared into the announcer's booth. Jeannie appeared to be laughing as she leaned forward and rubbed the filly on the neck.

As soon as the results were announced, the seven Adult Equitation riders were asked to trot their horses. Well, except for the gaited horse. She went into her running walk. After only half a lap around the large arena, the judge called for the riders to drop their stirrups. The lady on the gaited horse smiled broadly. Her horse, with her smooth gaits, was easy to ride without stirrups. The other riders had to continue posting to the trot. After another half lap, the judge asked for a collected, sitting trot. Everyone slowed down, except for one horse who was apparently unhappy that the stirrups were banging against his sides. It probably hadn't helped that his rider had been bouncing rather than posting. That horse just kept charging ahead at a fast, almost out-of-control trot. The judge asked the riders to pick up their stirrups and resume a regular posting trot.

Almost immediately, the judge asked for a walk when she saw the problem horse's continued agitation as the rider struggled to get her feet back in the stirrups. Once the rider finally accomplished that goal, and her horse's ears were no longer flattened back in anger, the judge called for a canter.

"This was fun to watch," I said to Autumn Rose, "but we should probably spend a few minutes in the warm-up area making sure our horses are not thinking it would be fun to stick our heads in the dirt the way that horse was plotting!"

Autumn Rose laughed and we turned away. However, we both looked back when the announcer called for a hand gallop. Everyone sped up, except for the problem horse. He was already going much faster than everyone else anyway.

"That poor woman isn't having a good day," Autumn Rose said.

"Actually, I think it would be fun to ride that horse," I said. "I mean, not in a horse show, but just to train on."

"Not me!" said Autumn Rose. "I like agreeable horses."

"Well, I do too, but challenges can be fun!" I said. "Like my first horse. She was definitely challenging, but I sure did learn a lot from her." The pretty little Palomino mare had been given to me when she was in bad shape, thin, and unfit. By the time I got her healthy and retrained, I had outgrown her. I hoped I would never outgrow Freckles. He was so tuned in to me and so much fun to ride!

Chapter 8 - Horse Show Morning

We had just enough time to make sure our horses were listening to us before the announcer called the Adult class to come in and line up. We turned back toward the in-gate and rode in. The twelve riders in our age group spread out around the arena. At least most of us did. A few were bunched up and chatting away. If they had been Jeannie's students, they'd have been met by a very unhappy redhead after the class.

When the winners of the Adult Equitation class were announced, Jeannie walked out with the blue ribbon. It was kind of funny. In the Pleasure class, she had been beaming over a sixth place finish, but with her Equitation win, she showed no change of expression at all. Equitation was judged on the rider. She had been out there to give her horse a good experience and didn't care at all about the color of the ribbon she won. I knew she'd care about our class results though, so I made sure my position was as close to ideal as I could make it.

Soon we were trotting our horses around the arena. The announcer called for a sitting trot, but never asked us to drop our stirrups, as the previous class had done. From the sitting trot, we were told to canter. The next command was to stop and back up. Then it was walk, reverse directions, and trot. This time the announcer did say, "Drop your irons." After going all the way around the arena, posting without stirrups, my thighs were screaming at me. We finally got to pick up our stirrups again before coming back to a walk. Then it was time to canter once again. Finally, the announcer said to trot and line up.

When the announcer called my number for first place, unlike Jeannie, I reacted. I smiled so big my face hurt as I rode forward out of the line-up. When Autumn Rose's number was called for second, I dropped my reins to clap for her!

Jeannie met us as we exited the arena with a smile on her face too. "Nice job, ladies," she said. "Now, get off their backs, loosen your girth, and lead them back to the trailer for a drink of water."

"Don't we have one more class?" I asked.

"Yes, but they have to set the jumps up after the twelve-and-under Equitation class, and that'll take a few minutes. It's going to be a long day for your horses. So give them breaks whenever you can."

My parents caught up with us as we walked back to the trailer. "Congratulations, Jeannie!" Dad said. "You and your students are showing 'em how it's done!"

"Thank you, Mr. Callahan. When you've got girls like these two, who *want* to learn, it makes it easy."

Autumn and I exchanged surprised glances. Jeannie wasn't usually this free with her compliments.

Mom was, though. "We're so proud of you, honey!" she said, hugging me after I got Freckles' bridle off.

"Thanks, Mom." I pulled the water bucket out of the trailer and started toward the hydrant.

"Let me get that," Dad said, taking the bucket from my hand. "Can't have you getting dirty."

"Dad, I'm not three. I can get a bucket of water without making a mess these days!"

"Yeah, but it makes me feel useful," he grinned. He turned to Autumn Rose and extended his hand for her bucket as well. When she hesitated, he said, "Otherwise, I'll be unbalanced."

She handed him the bucket.

As he walked away, he said in a goofy voice, "And I'm already a little unbalanced as it is. Just ask my daughter."

Autumn Rose looked at me, giggling again, while I rolled my eyes.

Jeannie walked back to us, leading her filly, whom she had unsaddled, then hosed off over at the livestock wash rack. "As soon as you two have both done the jumping part of your Hunter Hack class, I'm driving back out to the ranch to drop her off," she said, nodding toward the filly. "I'll get Sadie and her horse and pick up a different one of my training horses for the afternoon classes. So make sure you have everything you need out of the trailer."

Autumn Rose and I unhooked our hay bags from the trailer and tied them on the side of the empty livestock holding pen near where we were parked, putting a few brushes with them.

"Where are your Western boots and show clothes?" Jeannie asked. "You'll want to get changed during lunch break while I'm gone."

"Mine are in my parents' car," I said, while Autumn Rose jumped back up into the trailer tack room to get her change of clothes. She stepped out, arms full, and Mom instantly reached for her stuff.

"I'll take this over and put it in our car with Meghan's things," she said, as she hurried off.

Dad got back with the water buckets just then. After both horses showed zero interest in the water, he carried the buckets over to where our hay bags hung on the fence.

The Adult Hunter Hack class was being called into the arena by then, so we slipped off our horses' halters, put on their bridles, tightened their girths, and mounted up to go watch.

As we turned our horses away from the trailer, Jeannie asked, "So are you planning to tie your horses by their bridle reins while I'm gone or what?"

Without thinking, we had both left our halters hanging on the side of the trailer.

"Dad to the rescue again!" Dad said, untying the lead ropes and carrying the halters and ropes to our growing cache at the fence.

"Thanks, Dad!"

"Thanks, Mr. Callahan!"

Autumn Rose and I had spoken in stereo. He turned and bowed. "Your servant, my Queens," he said.

Chapter 8 - Horse Show Morning

Autumn Rose was clearly suppressing another giggle as we walked our horses back toward the in-gate where we could watch the class.

Jeannie observed, "With only two horses in the class, this will go quickly."

I noticed that the jumps were set up on opposite sides of the arena. "I thought you said the two jumps would be in a line," I said to Jeannie.

"Yeah. Well, normally they are. But this judge must've wanted something different," Jeannie said. "Let's see what they do."

The judge had both riders in a line-up at the end of the arena. The first rider walked forward, picked up a trot, trotted a circle, then put her horse into a left lead canter and approached the first jump. She continued around the far end on the left lead, then cantered back across the diagonal of the arena, changing leads in the center. She proceeded to the right around that end, past the judge and the other exhibitor, then jumped the second jump. From there she cantered straight to the far end of the arena, stopped, and backed up. She then trotted back to the line-up while the second exhibitor did the pattern.

"I've never seen it done that way before. This is an interesting judge," Jeannie observed.

We hurried over to the little warm-up area where we trotted our horses to loosen their muscles back up. We also did some bending and stopping to make sure they were listening. It was crowded with five other kids in our age group all trying to practice over the one schooling jump. Jeannie finally saw a gap in the action and told

Autumn Rose to go jump it. As she was approaching the jump, with Jeannie yelling reminders about eyes up and heels down, the announcer called for our class to enter the arena.

Jeannie turned to me and said, "Just go! Freckles doesn't need a warm-up fence. He will be perfectly fine without it."

There wasn't time anyway, so I didn't argue.

The announcer told us to line up at the far end of the arena, the way the last class had done. Autumn and I were on one end, with five other riders next to us. The judge walked to the middle of the line and gave us our instructions. We were to do the same pattern the adults had done, except we could choose to change leads by dropping to a trot rather than by doing a flying lead change if we wanted. She asked if there were any questions. There weren't.

The judge turned, pointed to Autumn Rose, and said, "We'll start at this end. As soon as the person beside you is finished, take your horse out of the line-up and start your pattern."

Autumn Rose looked nervous.

"Breathe!" I quietly reminded her.

She took a deep breath and walked forward. Her beautiful little mare trotted a medium-sized circle, picking up her left lead as asked, and cantered down toward the jump. I thought Sage might be wavering slightly, but I saw Autumn Rose clamp her legs on the mare's sides to push her forward. Sage straightened and cantered to the unfamiliar-looking obstacle, jumping it higher than necessary. Autumn Rose popped up out of the saddle a little, but wasn't in danger of falling.

It took me a second to realize they had landed on the wrong lead, but Autumn must have felt it right away because she dropped Sage to one step of a trot and went instantly back onto the correct lead. They proceeded around the far end and crossed the diagonal coming back toward me. At the center, Autumn Rose executed another perfect drop-to-a-trot change of leads and continued toward the second jump.

I could see the determination on her face as she cantered past. Her eyes were looking up and around the corner to the next jump and her legs were firmly pushing Sage forward. The closer they got to the jump, the deeper her heels went and they looked like a perfect picture from a book as they jumped it. A few strides later, she stopped and backed up, then trotted back toward the line. There weren't a lot of people in the grandstand, but most of them were applauding.

The look on Autumn Rose's face was adorable—half disbelieving and half triumphant!

As she came back into the line-up next to me, I gathered up my reins and trotted Freckles forward. We trotted part way around our circle before picking up the left lead. As soon as I pointed him toward the jump, his ears shot forward and I felt him start to build power. I took a firmer hold on my reins to prevent that power from turning into speed, focused my eyes on the fence at the far end of the arena, and dropped my weight so far into my heels I was wondering if they might hit the jump pole.

We continued at a canter and as he took off over the jump, I laid my outside leg on him to remind him to land on the correct lead. He did! Then it was on to the center of the arena where he gave me an energetic flying lead change, hopping slightly up into the air as if he had just cantered over a small log. We continued past the line-up and around the corner toward the second jump. Once again I got serious about "eyes up, heels down" and we sailed above the obstacle. Before reaching the far end, I asked for a stop, except I might have been a little too keen with my signals because he slid to a stop like the reining horse he was, then backed up with barely a touch of the reins. There was applause and also a little bit of laughter from the onlookers.

I let Freckles stand still for a few seconds, then gathered my reins up and trotted back to the line-up. When I pulled up next to Autumn Rose, I whispered, "Oops."

She tried not to laugh.

The horse next to me walked sluggishly out of line, not wanting to leave the safety of being with other horses. Once he got going though, he really got going. He rushed down toward the jump, got in too close to it before taking off, then popped up into the air like bread from a toaster. He landed on the wrong lead and stayed that way all the way around the corner. His rider must not have noticed, because she pulled him back to a trot as if she were doing a simple lead change and cantered off again on the same lead she had just been on. The pair raced around the next corner and popped up over the second jump. The horse continued in high gear, carrying her all the way around the far end of the arena before she could get him back to a stop. He grudgingly backed up about three steps before she trotted him back into line.

It was interesting watching the different horses and riders' styles and attitudes. One horse wouldn't jump until he had stopped, sniffed the obstacle, then circled around for a second try. Another zig-zagged up to each jump while his rider tried frantically to keep him from going around. Then he'd almost stop before jumping from a near standstill. That didn't look like any fun at all. Another cantered the whole pattern on his left lead. And the last horse to go made it clear that he had no intention of leaving all the other horses. His rider was kicking and pleading with him, trying to get him out of line. After an embarrassingly long time, the judge signaled to the ring steward who walked over and led the horse forward, giving his rider the momentum she needed to get started. Even so, the horse stopped at the first jump and simply refused to go over it. After three refusals, the judge shouted to the announcer to start the flat work.

We all went out on the rail. Then it was the usual: trot, walk, canter, both directions. I was proud of Freckles. He hadn't been "on the muscle" like he sometimes gets after jumping. I realized that he had had time to stand still while the other five horses did their patterns, which gave his heart rate time to come back down. That had really helped.

Finally, the results were announced. Freckles' number was called first and Sage's second!

We rode out of the arena to find not only my parents, but Autumn Rose's too. I started to introduce them, but Mom said, "Oh, honey, we've been talking all morning. The Ifaitas are practically old friends now. So you girls go take care of your horses while we get a picnic lunch ready."

As we tied our horses near their hay bags and then unsaddled, I said to Autumn Rose, "I've met your dad before, working around Jeannie's place, but this is the first time I've ever seen your Mom and, um..."

"Not what you expected?" she laughed.

"Well, I guess I was a little surprised," I admitted.

"Yeah, she grew up in Pennsylvania. She doesn't have a drop of Native American blood in her."

"But you..." I wasn't sure how to say this.

"But I look like a full-blood?" Autumn Rose finished for me, without a trace of annoyance in her voice.

"Well, yeah. You do. You've got that gorgeous thick black hair and that awesome complexion. You had me fooled."

"Does it matter?" she asked.

"What do you mean?" I asked, puzzled.

"Does it matter whether I'm half one and half the other?" she asked.

"Well no, of course not. Why would it matter?"

"I don't have a clue. But to some people, it does."

"People are weird," I said.

Autumn Rose laughed. "Especially us!" she said happily.

I looked at her questioningly.

"We spend all of our time with animals, teaching them to do silly stuff, like jump over an obstacle when they can *see* it would be easier to go around it," she said.

"Yeah," I agreed. "And isn't it *fun*?!"

"Well, the jumping part wasn't, at least not at first! But once a friend reminds you to breathe—and you do—it actually *is* fun! And I never thought I'd say that," Autumn admitted.

I laughed out loud. "I know! If anyone had told me a year ago that I would be showing Freckles English, I'd have told them they were crazy. But here we are. And I'm having a blast!"

Half a Saddle Off

Chapter 9
One Angry Redhead

Jeannie returned as we were finishing lunch. While she and Sadie unloaded their horses, I grabbed my Western show clothes out of Mom and Dad's car and climbed into the trailer tack room to change. When I checked my makeup, I realized my hair was still up under a hairnet for fitting under my English helmet. I peeled off the net, pulled out the hair clips, undid the band, and shook my hair loose. After a few swipes with my hairbrush, I rebraided my hair, then turned it into a tight bun at the base of my neck so I could put my cowboy hat on without it being in the way.

While I was trying to corral my unruly hair, Jeannie saddled up and rode off toward the arena to warm up her training horse. This one was a chestnut color too, but where the filly had been petite and dainty-looking, this was a stud colt, three years old and heavily muscled. Meanwhile, Sadie was hard at work brushing Deluxe's already-shining dark brown coat and spraying something into his black mane and tail to make them even shinier.

To my surprise, I noticed that Autumn Rose had finished regrooming her horse and had moved over to brush Freckles off too. As I finished with my hair, she was untying Freckles and leading him to the trailer for me.

"I'm starting to feel like I have my own personal groom," I said.

"I owed you," she said, pointing to her hair, which was still in under-the-helmet mode, as mine had been. "Anything else?"

"No, but thanks. I just need to find my Showmanship halter and put a little baby oil on him," I said.

"You've got your show clothes on; let me do the baby oil," she said, handing me Freckles' lead rope and hopping into the trailer tack room. She popped out with my leather halter and matching lead shank, which she handed me. She then opened the oil jar and carefully rubbed some around Freckles' eyes and muzzle while I stayed clean and tidy. I even managed to get the leather halter on his head without getting any oil on me.

"Where's your number?" Autumn asked.

"Oh, I forgot. It's still on the back of my hunt coat. It's in my parents' car." She ran over, unpinned it, and brought it back.

"Turn around," she ordered.

"You're not mad at me for beating you in the Hunter Hack are you?" I asked.

"What?" she started to say, but then caught on. "Don't make me laugh or I *will* stab you with one of these pins."

I kept my mouth shut and she got my number pinned to the back of my shirt without drawing blood.

"It's even practically straight," she said, standing back to look at the number. "Upside down, but straight."

"No! You didn't—" I turned my back toward Sadie. "Sadie, is my number on okay?"

She looked over from where she was buckling Deluxe's silver-plated halter onto his head and said, "Yeah. It's on right."

Autumn Rose laughed.

The announcer gave a first call for the Adult Showmanship class and told those still warming their horses up that they needed to vacate the arena.

"I'll be cheering you both on!" said Autumn Rose as Sadie and I started toward the warm-up area, leading our horses.

Sadie flashed her brilliant smile Autumn Rose's way, while I simply mumbled, "Thanks."

This was definitely my least favorite class of the day. I only entered it because Jeannie said it was necessary if I were to have a chance at winning the All-Around Championship. I led Freckles over toward the in-gate, where I could watch the competitors in the adult class. Most of the women—there were no men in the class —were wearing fancy, brightly-colored, fitted western blouses that sparkled with sequins. A few wore tailored western jackets with matching pants like Sadie's. Only two of them were dressed as plainly as I was in my off-the-rack western shirt and blue jeans.

After all the exhibitors had led their horses at least halfway around the arena, the announcer called for them to line up. Starting at one end of the line-up, the ring steward pointed to each person, one at a time, signaling them to start the pattern. Each, in turn, was to lead her horse out of line to an orange cone where she would stop her horse, back him or her up six steps, do a 360 degree turn to the left, then trot toward the judge.

About a horse's length in front of the judge, the rider was to stop, square the horse up so that the front and hind feet formed a perfect rectangle, then look at the judge. At this point, the judge would walk around the horse while the handler positioned herself where she could keep an eye on the judge while simultaneously staying out of the judge's line-of-sight as the judge looked her horse over. If the judge was anywhere around the front half of her horse, she stood on the opposite side of her horse's head from the judge. But when the judge was around the horse's hindquarters, she would step to the same side as the judge. It all seemed like some weird dance. Once the judge excused the handler, she was to trot her horse straight back to the cone where she had started, set her horse up squarely for a few seconds, then, when the judge nodded to her, take her horse back into the line-up.

Chapter 9 - One Angry Redhead

I walked over to where the Showmanship pattern for my class was hanging on the fence. I was glad to see it was the same pattern. There was nothing there that we couldn't do.

Then I looked around for Sadie. She was over in the warm-up area, practicing the pattern. The sunlight was reflecting off the silver in Deluxe's halter and off of his haircoat as well. He was unbelievably shiny-looking. And Sadie looked fabulous in her tailored outfit.

The announcer called our class into the arena while waiting for the judge to send up the results for the Adult Showmanship. I led Freckles in with the fifteen other exhibitors, and we went through the whole process that the adults had done. It seemed to go on forever. When it was our turn, Freckles did everything pretty correctly, though he didn't respond to my cues as quickly as he sometimes did. I guess he was bored too.

When the announcer finally clicked the microphone on, it was Sadie's number he announced in first place. Freckles and I placed sixth.

We walked out of the arena to see Jeannie congratulating Sadie. I didn't think she'd bother to congratulate me. However, I was truly surprised when I heard the ice-cold tone of her voice when she said my name.

"Meghan!"

I stopped Freckles and looked into the eyes of a distinctly unhappy redhead, which, to be honest, is a somewhat frightening sight.

"If that's all the effort you're going to put into the rest of your classes today, then you can just go tie your horse to the trailer and ask your parents to take you home." Her voice came out almost as a hiss.

I didn't know what to say. I'd never seen her that mad unless she was talking to her ex-husband. I looked down at the green ribbon in my hand.

Almost as if she had read my mind, she said, "I don't care about the color of that ribbon! I care that you put almost zero effort into that class. You slumped through it as if you were embarrassed to be out there. And it was obvious you hadn't bothered to tune your horse in to you before you did your pattern. How dare you do such a disservice to your horse!" She paused for breath, then continued. "Now you either go home or go saddle him up and actually turn your brain back on. Freckles deserves a *rider*, not some unfocused kid who doesn't care about her horse!"

Jeannie spun on her heel and walked back toward the trailer where her colt was tied.

I stood still, as if my feet were suddenly stuck to the ground. Emotions were swirling around inside of me, screaming for attention. I was angry. I was embarrassed. I was frustrated. So what if I hadn't done as well in the class as Jeannie thought I should? She knew I was paying for my show clothes out of my own pocket. I couldn't afford the fancy Showmanship suit that Sadie's parents had bought, or the fancy silver-plated halter either. How was I supposed to compete against that?

I glanced around me. Who else had heard Jeannie's tirade? Some of the other exhibitors in my age group had clearly heard her. Some were smirking at me. Some looked away as soon as we made eye contact, pretending they hadn't listened to her humiliate me.

I nearly jumped out of my skin as I felt a hand on my arm. I turned to find Autumn Rose looking up at me. "Are you okay?" she asked unnecessarily.

"Obviously not," I said, still angry.

"You need to be," she said.

Her comment surprised me. "Huh, what…what do you mean?" I stammered.

"Your horse needs you," she said simply. She turned, pulling lightly on my arm, and started toward the trailer.

I broke loose and walked, somewhat woodenly, beside her.

Jeannie had untied her horse, mounted up, and ridden away before we got back to the trailer.

"She only gets mad like that because she cares," Autumn Rose said quietly, "and she knows what you and Freckles are capable of accomplishing."

My brain, which was still trying to wrap itself around all my crazy emotions, suddenly zeroed in on Autumn Rose's words.

"Shut your eyes, Meghan, and take a deep breath. Now picture Threepio this morning. After he got bucked off the stud horse, he shook the dirt off his feet and left his trouble behind him. You need to do the same."

I looked at Autumn Rose, wanting to say, "Thank you," but knowing I'd cry if I tried to speak.

She reached over and grabbed Freckles' lead shank out of my hand, then, smiling, she said, "If you think I'm saddling this giant beast for you, you can forget it. I owed you for fixing my hair this morning—but not *that* much. Go do it yourself."

I turned toward the trailer tack room, took two steps, and heard her say, "One more thing: as a wise person once told me—"

I turned back.

"Breathe. Just breathe."

I actually smiled. And breathed.

After Freckles placed third in the Western Pleasure class, I walked him out the gate and congratulated Sadie on her win.

She smiled and said, "I told you you'd be riding for second. Well, third." She giggled as she walked away toward the warm-up area.

Remembering Autumn Rose's advice, I took a deep breath. Sadie's comment wasn't worth getting annoyed over. I needed to focus on my horse, not be distracted by Sadie. I took Freckles to the warm-up area also. First, I just let him walk and relax. Then as our next class got closer, I started doing little things to make sure he was listening. I asked him for a super-slow jog, then went straight into a backup and, after six steps, put him into a lope.

He was listening, yet relaxed, just the way I wanted him as we walked into the arena to start the Western Horsemanship class. I stretched up to my full height, sitting as straight and tall as possible.

Once again, the judge hadn't asked for a pattern. She had us do the usual walk-jog-lope to the left, but then asked us to stop our horses. While stopped, she asked for a reverse, but she specified it was to be a turn-on-the-haunches. I had to think for a minute. Reverses were always done toward the inside of the arena, and if you were walking when they called for a reverse, you were to continue walking or if jogging, continue jogging. So, I signaled Freckles as if we were starting a spin to the left, but then stopped him almost immediately. It worked! We had done a 180-degree turn on the haunches.

I noticed that some riders were turning toward the fence. Some were turning and walking away. I wasn't sure which was the right thing to do. The judge then asked everyone to jog their horses, and after halfway around the arena, asked us to stop and back up. That was one of the exercises we'd been doing during warm-up, so I was sure Freckles would do it perfectly. And he did. While we were still backing, the judge called for a lope. I backed him one more step, pushing his hip to the inside, then loped off on the correct lead.

Soon, the judge told us to jog our horses again, and I used my weight and my hands to bring Freckles back into a jog, but I had my legs ready to squeeze in case he misunderstood and tried to walk or stop. While we were still jogging, the judge told us to pick up the wrong lead, "also known as a counter canter or false lead," she clarified.

Freckles and I were just coming into the corner at the end of the long side of the arena. I asked him for the counter canter, but he was confused. He couldn't quite believe that I wanted him to take a left lead when there was a right-hand corner in front of us. Rather than respond immediately, as he usually did, he took an extra half step and went off onto the right lead, which would normally have been correct. But I had asked him for the left. I brought him back to a jog and asked again, just as we approached the second right-hand corner on that end of the arena. Freckles wrung his tail in annoyance, then stepped into the right lead again, which, in this case, was again the wrong one.

I brought him back to a jog as we came out of the turn and started down the long straightaway. This time, when I asked for the left lead, he finally got it.

We loped down the long side, with me feeling rattled at our two errors. As we approached the next corner, we made number three. I felt Freckles make a small hop, as he executed a flying lead change, putting himself back on what he believed was the correct lead. Before I could pull him up and fix it, the judge told us to walk and come to the center. There she asked us each to dismount and mount back up.

Chapter 9 - One Angry Redhead

I focused my attention on the details of doing everything precisely and as correctly as I possibly could.

After the judge had sent her results up to the announcer, she walked back over to me and said, "You had the class won until you blew your counter canter."

As she walked away, I heard the announcer say that Sadie had won the class. Freckles and I placed fourth.

Walking out of the arena, I saw Jeannie waiting for me. I steeled myself for another tongue-lashing. To my surprise, she said, "You rode beautifully." As she turned her colt away to go back to the warm-up arena, she added, "Remind me next week, and we'll work on false leads."

I dismounted and walked over to the signboard to double check my pattern for the Reining class, my brain squirming around like a bucket of hot worms. I had messed up, yet Jeannie was proud of me. The judge, too, had apparently liked everything except our counter canter mistakes. I was so confused. But I knew I had to focus on the next event, so I consciously shoved everything else out of my head.

Fortunately, the Reining pattern was one I knew, but just to be certain, I reviewed every single step. Then I walked back and looked at the arena, picturing exactly where I'd be for each maneuver. By then, it was time to warm up. I did the same sort of tune-ups I had done for the Horsemanship class, so that Freckles was listening and light. This was my very favorite class. It would be fun.

And it was! I totally focused on clear communication between Freckles and me, and by the time we had finished our figure eights, spins, rollbacks, stop and back up, I was smiling so big that my face hurt. Again. After the final maneuver, I became aware of noise coming from the grandstand. My parents, no doubt. I looked up, surprised to see a small group of people cheering and whistling. My folks were a part of it, but leading the noise was Autumn Rose and *her* parents! And as I rode out of the arena, Jeannie looked to be just this side of giddy.

"That was *so* much fun!" I said, before she even opened her mouth.

"It was fun to watch too!" she agreed. "You can be real proud of your horse and yourself!"

I watched the other reiners go, but I was surprised when Sadie's number was announced as a "scratch." For some reason, she had decided not to compete.

When Freckles' number was named the winner, our little fan club erupted in cheers again. The group hurried down out of the grandstand. Mom and Dad both hugged me. Autumn Rose hugged Freckles. Autumn Rose's parents both shook my hand.

Jeannie rode by and said, "I hate to break this up, but they just announced that the Trail Class will be closing in twenty minutes, so if you haven't done it yet, you better get over there."

I led Freckles over to where the Trail course had been set up and looked over the pattern. Once I had it in my head, I looked around at each individual obstacle and pictured us going through it in the correct order at the proper speeds. Then I mounted and retuned Freckles before riding to the in-gate, where I asked the judge—a different judge from the main arena—if it was okay for me to start. He asked for my number, then wrote it down on a score sheet.

I continued to watch him. When he finally looked up from his clipboard and nodded, I rode Freckles to the in-gate, opened it, side-passed through, then pushed it shut and latched it behind us. From there, we jogged to a bridge, came back to a walk, and walked over the center of it. Freckles really looked hard at it. I wondered if he was trying to see if it was going to rock the way the last one had.

After stepping off the bridge, we loped to a pole on the ground next to a mailbox. I stopped Freckles at the end of the pole and side-passed over the pole to the mailbox. I bent down, pulled a letter out, waved it at the judge, then put it back in and closed the box.

Once we had side-passed over the pole and away from the mailbox, we walked a few steps to two barrels, stepped between them and stopped. On top of one was an old grain sack full of aluminum cans. I picked it up with my free hand and passed it across to set it down on top of the other barrel. The cans made a lot of noise, but Freckles wasn't bothered by them at all.

From there we jogged to a line of cones and wove between them. Almost immediately, we stopped and backed through a dogleg, a narrow alleyway made of ground poles, with almost a right angle turn at the halfway point. Freckles backed through carefully, never touching a pole with any of his feet.

I looked over at the judge and smiled. He nodded back, and I walked out of the arena.

"That was easy compared to the stuff Jeannie's been making us practice over," I said as I dismounted.

"You certainly made it look easy," Autumn Rose's mother said.

"Where's Autumn Rose?" I asked.

"She's saddling up for the Barrel Racing and Polebending," her mother answered.

Dad asked, in mock excitement, "Are you in that too, Meghan? I've always wanted to see you race a barrel!"

"Um, no, Dad," I said distractedly. "And I didn't know Autumn Rose was going to try it!"

Her mother laughed. "She loves Barrel Racing! That's what her mare was doing before she got her."

I think I must've looked like a fish face for about ten seconds while I closed, then opened, then closed my mouth, totally unable to form words.

Finally, a couple of brain cells resumed working and I managed to say, "I need to get Freckles taken care of so I can go cheer Autumn Rose and Sage on!"

Mom and Dad helped in whatever little ways they could, and I soon had Freckles unsaddled, brushed off, watered, and tied to the trailer, his nose happily stuffed into his hay bag.

146

Chapter 9 - One Angry Redhead

While my parents went back up into the grand-stand, I changed out of my nice show shirt into a T-shirt, then took my hair out of the bun and brushed it out. By the time I joined them in the stands, the arena crew was setting the barrels in the familiar triangular pattern.

Mom handed me a water bottle and a container of strawberries. She's kinda awesome sometimes.

"This is like that event we saw at the rodeo in Colorado, isn't it?" Mom asked.

"Yeah, where they run sort of a cloverleaf pattern around the barrels and the fastest time wins," Dad said, clearly happy to sound as if he knew what he was talking about. "Oh yeah, and if they knock over a barrel, they get time added to their score."

"Well done, Dad," I said. "You win a strawberry."

"Thanks," he said, and picked one out of my container.

The first junior contestant's number was called and the class began. I was only half-paying attention, because I didn't know any of the younger riders. But Mom and Dad both appeared to be delighted, watching the little ones. Some of the kids couldn't quite control their horses well enough to get through the pattern. They would run in, go around or even past the first barrel, then run back to the gate. But at least they were out there trying. One little girl was able to do the whole pattern on her antique pony, who never went faster than a slow jog. A few were pretty good. In fact, one little girl was so fast, I wondered if I would have had the courage to do what she was doing when I was her age.

Finally, the last of the junior riders finished, and it was time for Sadie and Autumn Rose's class.

Chapter 10
Timed Events

The first contestant in Barrel Racing was fast, but knocked down a barrel, earning a five-second penalty. The second rider didn't have to worry about knocking any of the barrels down because she never got close to them. Her turns were so big that her time was even slower than the girl who'd had the time-added penalty. The third entry looked fast between the barrels, but the rider was really jerking on her horse's mouth to get him to slow down and turn. Plus, she was leaning in toward the barrels so hard that her horse had to lean out away from them to counterbalance her. Even so, she had the fastest time so far.

One thing I noticed that they all had in common was how they stretched their legs out as wide as they could and used them to kick and spur their horses after they came around the last barrel and headed for the gate.

That seemed weird to me because my first trainer, Ol' Ben, had always said, "If you wanna speed yer horse up, hit him on the butt. That's where his engine is," or "Spurs are fer turnin', not fer speed. If you kick him in the belly, he's not gonna wanna stretch out an' run. He's gonna put his energy into wringin' his tail and flattenin' his ears to tell ya he's not happy." That's what the horse in the arena at the moment was doing: wringing his tail so he looked almost like a helicopter. And his ears were flat back, making it clear that he was seriously annoyed.

I could still hear Ben's voice in my head. "If you're smart, you'll listen to him. Otherwise, you end up with a horse that doesn't wanna give you his best. Shucks, some of 'em get so 'ring sour' they don't want to go into an arena at all, 'cause they know they're just gonna get hurt."

I heard them call Sadie's number as being on deck, so I knew she'd be going after the next horse. But the next horse was still outside the arena, rearing and spinning away from the gate. Finally a man grabbed the horse by the bridle and led him into the arena. They would've had a pretty fast time if they hadn't knocked down the last barrel. Like the other riders, this girl was spurring him hard to make him run, but she was also hitting him with a short length of rope on his rump. As soon as they crossed the finish line, the girl stood in her stirrups and leaned back, yanking on her horse's mouth with everything she had, trying to get him to stop.

It was really hard to watch.

Sadie's big bay horse, Hobo, came into the arena willingly and got straight to work. Sadie was using her spurs, I noticed, but at least her hands were good. There was no jerking and tearing on her horse's mouth as so many of the others had done. She did some heavy-duty spurring on the final part of the run, but then circled Hobo to slow him down rather than trying to yank him to a stop.

We all applauded for her, and then applauded even louder when her time was announced. She was firmly in the lead!

The next rider tried too hard to catch Sadie and knocked down two barrels.

Then it was Autumn Rose's turn. Sage walked into the arena, head down and relaxed.

Dad leaned toward me and whispered, "She *does* know this is a timed event, right?"

Despite his attempt to be quiet, Autumn Rose's mother overhead him and started laughing. "Oh, she knows. She'll be burnin' and turnin' in just a few seconds. Just watch!"

We watched.

Autumn Rose shortened her reins a little and signaled Sage for a right lead canter. Sage started off slowly into a circle, but by the time they came out of the circle and headed toward the starting line, she was running faster than I'd ever seen her go. At the first barrel, Autumn Rose sat deeper into her saddle, her weight slightly to the outside of the turn, and eased her mare through the turn. Then she stood up in her stirrups and leaned forward, heading for the next barrel and a left-hand turn. They zipped around it and headed for the third barrel. They were barely out of the final turn when Autumn Rose stood up in what Jeannie would've called "two-point position," if she'd been in an English saddle, and raced across the finish line. Autumn Rose sat back down in the saddle and Sage slowed, as she spiraled into a circle, finally dropping to a walk.

We were all on our feet by then, cheering. When the announcer clicked the microphone on and said, "New leader, by five-tenths of a second," we got a whole lot louder!

I ran down out of the grandstand to where Autumn Rose was walking Sage around the warm-up area.

"That was amazing!" I told her.

Autumn Rose smiled, then dropped her eyes. "Oh, I don't know about that. But it sure was fun."

Sadie trotted past and I called out to her, "Nice ride, Sadie!"

She turned and shot me a look that was so full of venom that I actually took a step back. I glanced at Autumn Rose, but she was checking her girth. I didn't think she'd seen Sadie's look, so I didn't say anything to her about it.

"Do you need anything? Water? Food?" I asked.

"No, I'm good," Autumn Rose answered. "But thanks."

"I think I'll go back up to the stands then," I said and hurried off before Sadie came back around the loop.

They were announcing the placings as I approached the grandstands. No one had beaten Autumn's or Sadie's times, so they had placed first and second. Autumn Rose's parents passed me on their way down to congratulate their daughter.

"She sure did an amazing job," I said as we passed.

Her mom surprised me by stopping to say, "You've been a good friend to our daughter. We appreciate you, Meghan."

Before I could think how to respond, she turned and hurried after her husband.

I walked back up to where Mom and Dad were still sitting. "I don't have any more classes, you know."

Mom looked puzzled for a minute, then laughed. "You mean, why are we still here?"

"Well, sort of. I just know it's been a long day of sitting and watching. You don't have to stick around. I'll ride back to the barn with Jeannie after the Polebending, and I'll call you when we get the horses taken care of. You two can take off whenever you want."

"We will, honey. But we've been having so much fun getting acquainted with Autumn Rose's parents that we haven't been in a hurry to leave. They're interesting people," Mom said.

"Besides," Dad said, "I want to see people bend poles. That's gotta take a lot of strength."

As usual, Dad said it as if he were serious, but I was fairly sure he was just being goofy. Even so, I thought I should try to explain it to him. "So actually, Dad, in Polebending, a series of poles is set up; the riders run their horses to the far end of the arena past the last pole, then weave back between the poles, then back through the other direction, and run to the finish line."

"So they're actually weaving the poles?" he asked.

"Yes."

"I've heard of weaving with yarn, but poles have to be tough…"

"Daaaaddddd," I said in exasperation.

"What?" he said with his most innocent expression.

"Oh, just watch the class. You'll see how it's done."

In the arena, the volunteers were taking out the barrels and were setting the poles in place.

The announcer was reading the results for the adult Barrel class just as Autumn Rose's parents came back up into the stands to sit with us. When he named the winner, he also repeated her winning time.

"Wow!" I said. "Autumn Rose's time was faster than the winner of this last class."

Her mother beamed. Her father said, "She's worked hard to help that mare understand her job."

To my relief, Dad didn't make any more dorky remarks.

The men started talking about woodworking and the women about their jobs. Autumn Rose's mom was a nurse and mine was a dental assistant, and those two jobs apparently had some similar frustrations.

Anyway, I zoned out watching the little kids Pole-bending.

Finally, it was time for the Intermediate riders. This time Autumn Rose drew up earlier in the group than Sadie. Once again, Sage walked into the arena as if she were going for a stroll in the park. But after Autumn Rose put her into a lope, she was soon racing for the far end of the arena. Once they passed the last pole, they spun around it, then darted back and forth between the poles as smoothly as I'd ever seen. After they rounded the final pole, they ran for the finish line and the announcer called the time. It was much faster than any of the junior riders had done, but I wasn't sure it would hold up against all the intermediate-age riders.

Sadie had drawn up as the final rider and she came into the arena looking as if she were breathing fire. She sent Hobo at a dead run for the far end, then wove the poles with some serious power. When they rounded the last pole, Sadie was whipping and spurring with everything she had.

That had been smokin' fast. So I was really surprised when the announcer called her time: two-tenths of a second slower than Autumn Rose. Sage had beaten Hobo again! Wow!

"That was amazing," I heard Dad say. "Your daughter's run didn't appear to be as fast because it was so smooth. But she really nailed it! Let's all go congratulate her!"

As we all stood up, I heard Autumn Rose's mom say, "We need to congratulate Sadie, too. She had a good run."

I was pretty sure Sadie wouldn't be anywhere near the gate. And I was right. We all gathered around Sage, telling her what a good girl she was and telling Autumn Rose her ride had been brilliant. But Sadie was nowhere to be seen.

Autumn Rose's and my parents left immediately after she picked up her blue ribbon. She dismounted, loosened her girth, and walked Sage back to the trailer.

I walked along beside her, not sure how to say what I needed to say. "Autumn Rose," I started, "um, I think Sadie might be a little, um, unpleasant, on the drive home."

"Well, I doubt she will be much more unpleasant than she has already been," Autumn Rose said.

"Oh. So you noticed she wasn't happy about being beaten."

"Would've been hard to miss," Autumn Rose responded. "But, Meghan, that's not my problem. And I'm not going to take it personally, no matter what Sadie says. She's upset at getting beaten. I understand that. I used to get upset too. And I used those feelings to drive myself to become a better competitor—that is to say, a better horsewoman."

"Yeah… about that. I've never seen you practice barrels or poles," I said. "So, um, how did you go out there today and do so incredibly well?!" I demanded.

Autumn Rose laughed. "I homeschool. Remember? I was practicing in the mornings, when it was cool, and only riding English when you rode after *your* school got out."

We got back to the trailer in time to see Jeannie loading her colt into the front space. I pulled the saddle off Sage and stowed it in the tack room, then untied Freckles and loaded him into the trailer. By then Sage was haltered and ready to load. I grabbed my water bucket, dumped it, and then untied my empty hay bag from the side of the trailer. Both went into the trailer tack room while Sadie loaded her horses.

Sadie climbed into the front seat of the truck, while Autumn Rose and I squashed ourselves into the back. My knees were about in my chin. Fortunately, it wasn't a long drive.

Jeannie talked the whole way back to the barn about how happy she was with how her training horses had handled their first big outing; about how pleased she was at how Autumn Rose and I had done in the English classes; about how well Sadie had done in the Showmanship. She actually looked back over her shoulder at me when she said that, then added she was *certain* I would do better next time. Then she complimented Sadie again, this time for her Western Pleasure and Horsemanship wins. To my surprise, she said she had been proud of me in those two classes too, and promised, again that we would work on picking up false leads before the next show.

"And your reining pattern was gorgeous, Meghan. You would have placed well against the adults here today. And that's going some because we have a lot of good reiners in this area," Jeannie said. Then she surprised me when she asked if any of us had heard the results for the Trail Class. I had gotten so sidetracked watching the timed events that I had completely forgotten about Trail. So I hadn't heard. Apparently Sadie hadn't either.

"I didn't think so," said Jeannie, "so I stopped off at the secretary's booth and picked up the first and second place ribbons you two girls won."

"Congratulations, Sadie," I said, assuming I'd been 'riding for second' as I usually was against her.

"Actually no, Meghan. Sadie should be congratulating you. You and Freckles won the Trail," Jeannie said. "I looked at the judge's comments on the placings. You two were essentially tied for first place, but the judge wrote that you, Meghan, looked like you were really enjoying yourself out there. That's what put you over the top."

To my total lack of surprise, Sadie did not congratulate me.

"And, oh my word," Jeannie continued, to have you two go first and second in the timed events was super cool. Even though I don't actually coach either one of you on your speed classes, most people don't realize that, so your success reflects well on my barn."

Chapter 10 - Timed Events

I don't think I had ever realized you could sense someone else's tension and anger before, but it seemed to be positively boiling up out of the front seat where Sadie sat, arms folded across her chest and fists clenched tightly.

Jeannie continued, oblivious to Sadie's mounting anger. "After this show, you're well in the lead for the Intermediate All-Around Championship, Meghan. In fact, you girls all did so well today that I spent most of the afternoon talking to parents about the possibility of teaching their kids and training their horses. So thank you all!"

As Jeannie turned into Sadie's driveway, she asked, "Are you going over to Meghan's house again tonight?"

"No!" Sadie said through tight lips and a clenched jaw. "My aunt and uncle are arriving tonight from Texas to stay with us for a week. So I don't need to be *babysat.*"

While Sadie and Jeannie unloaded Deluxe and Hobo, Autumn Rose and I got Sadie's bridles, saddle blankets, brushes, buckets, and hay bags out of the trailer and carried them into her barn. Sadie swept past us without so much as a "Thanks" and grabbed her fancy show saddle. I picked up her barrel racing saddle and followed her back into the barn. She placed her silver-plated saddle on its rack, then turned and jerked Hobo's saddle out of my hands.

"I thought you were supposed to be my friend," she snarled before turning her back on me.

"I thought I was too," I said. "In fact, I still think I am."

"Well, think again, 'cause you're *not.*"

I turned and walked out of her barn.

Later, after we'd unloaded the horses and put our saddles away, I walked out to check Freckles' water bucket. It was full.

Threepio had followed me, so I scooped him up, cuddled him, and burst into tears. He wrapped his paws gently around my neck, purring.

Autumn Rose's voice surprised me as she walked up behind me. "Are you okay?"

I couldn't answer at that particular moment so I just sort of hid my face in Threepio's fur.

"I heard her," Autumn Rose said simply. Then she waited in silence.

"Not gonna lie," I admitted when I could finally speak without blubbering. "That stung. We've been friends for nearly a year. At least I thought we were."

"You realize it's not you that she's actually mad at, don't you?" Autumn Rose asked.

"Oh, I'd have to say Sadie was pretty clear about who she's mad at."

"Except she's not," Autumn Rose insisted. "Sadie's mad at herself for not working as hard as you did preparing for the show. She's not stupid. She knows she messed up. But it's easier to take it out on you rather than own up to her personal failures."

I thought about that for a couple of minutes. Finally, I asked, "Do you really think so?"

"Well, no one can really know what's in another person's head, but that's sure what it seems like," she said. "So try not to take it personally, no matter how personal it felt."

I wasn't sure I'd be able to sleep, even though I was seriously tired when I went to bed that night. But I made an intentional decision to set down the hurt I'd picked up from Sadie and not pick it back up.

I was asleep within minutes.

For the next week, things were pretty peaceful at the barn. Jeannie said that Sadie was too busy with her aunt and uncle to come for lessons, so it was just Autumn Rose and me all week. I felt kinda guilty, as relieved as I was at not having to put up with Sadie's moods.

Jeannie suddenly had a lot of new students, too, but they rode at different times than Autumn Rose and I did.

As promised, one of the main things Jeannie worked Freckles and me on was how to take a false lead. It wasn't really all that hard, once she explained it. It was just weird setting him up for a particular lead when you were going the wrong direction for it. I finally had to pretend the arena fence was on the inside, toward the center of the arena. That enabled me to "see" in my head how I was supposed to be using my aids. Once I got my legs, hands, and weight right, Freckles took the lead I wanted every time, whether a false lead or a correct one, even on the corners.

Encouraging him to keep a false lead around the corner wasn't too hard either, once I learned to drop my weight to the inside slightly and slide my inside leg back a little, pushing his hip to the outside.

"It's all about balance," Jeannie said. And slowly I began to feel when the balance was correct.

⌇

"I'd like to try another sleepover," I said at dinner one evening.

"Well sure," Mom said hesitantly, "but this time, would you please ask her to leave her cell phone home?"

"No, not Sadie," I said. "This time I want to invite Autumn Rose."

My parents both suddenly looked much more favorable toward the idea.

"Sure!" Mom said. "When are you thinking?"

"Maybe this Friday, if that works for her."

⌇

Autumn Rose managed to get a "yes" from her parents about the sleepover, so Friday, after we'd finished with our horses and our chores at the barn, Dad showed up to drive us home. He picked up Autumn's overnight bag and put it in the back of the SUV; then, acting like a chauffeur, he opened the car door for her and bowed. She climbed in, giggling.

"So, what's the deal?" I complained. "I have to open my car door myself?"

"Yep!" he said cheerfully, climbing into the driver's seat, while I opened my own door and got into the passenger side of the back seat as Autumn Rose laughed harder.

On the way home, she actually talked to my dad, surprising me with her questions.

"Your job keeps your family on the move, much like my mother's job, doesn't it?" she asked.

"Yes it does, although I don't think we move as often as you do. In fact, if you stick around, I bet you'll get to enjoy my darling daughter's company for at least another year here," he said.

That's something I hadn't known.

She kept asking him questions about his work, and by the time we pulled into our driveway, I knew more about Dad's job than I'd ever known before.

Dinner went the same way. Autumn Rose was talking to them as if she were an adult. And they were answering her, not treating her like one of my "little friends," as Dad had called Sadie. It was kind of amazing to listen to.

After dinner, Autumn Rose and I helped with the clean-up until Mom chased us out of the kitchen, saying she was sure we had more fun things to do than kitchen work.

We went up to my room and started talking. And laughing. For hours!

About midnight, she was telling me about Sage and how she had saved up her money and bought her from a girl who was trying to compete in barrel racing and polebending on her. But Sage hadn't understood her job. She was consistently knocking over the barrels and the poles, and the girl was always calling the mare stupid.

"I knew that wasn't true. You could see the intelligence in her eyes. And I could see that she's a kind horse too. Any other horse would've bucked that girl off."

I laughed at the idea of sweet Sage bucking, then asked, "How did you turn her into such a success?"

"It was about that time I met the dressage instructor in Farmington," Autumn Rose said. "She watched me riding Sage one day and offered to help me with her."

"That doesn't sound like a typical English trainer, taking an interest in a barrel horse, I mean."

"I don't think you could call her a typical anything. She has been a jockey, an artist, a model, and who knows what else," Autumn Rose laughed. "She told me she gets bored easily."

"Apparently!"

"She thought Sage and I would be a 'fun challenge,' so she started teaching me how to use my legs and my weight to bend and balance her. Sage responded really well."

"She must have," I said, replaying her Polebending run in my head. "The way she seemed to slip between the poles at the show was unreal. It didn't look as if you were going all that fast, but it was so slick, no one could catch you!"

"Well, it didn't hurt that she also worked on me to lengthen Sage's stride. Some horses *look* as if they're going fast because they're taking a lot of short steps. Sage covers more ground with fewer steps. Kind of like you do with your long legs."

I nodded, beginning to understand.

"She also taught me how I should ride so I don't mess her stride up."

"How do you mean?"

"Well, in order to run fast, a horse has to lengthen her body out. If the rider is poking her with spurs, she can't," Autumn Rose said. "I mean, think about it: If you were trying to stretch up to get something off the top shelf, and you knew someone was going to walk up behind you and poke you in the ribs, would you stretch out as far as you could?"

"No! I'd be scrunched down trying to protect myself," I said.

"It's the same for the horse, she can't stretch out and run if someone is poking her with spurs every step or knocking the wind out of her by kicking as hard as they can. Spurs don't make a horse go faster. If they did, my trainer said she'd have figured out how to wear spurs when she was a jockey."

"Ben always said the motor's in the back, so if you want speed, that's where you put the pressure," I said.

"But there's more to getting top speed than that," Autumn Rose said.

"Like what?" I asked.

"Like not touching your backside down onto the horse's back while running."

"How do you mean?"

"When my instructor was a jockey, she learned that every time a jockey's seat touches the horse's back when the horse is running flat out, it throws the horse slightly off stride, shortening the stride and slowing the horse. When you're dealing with a matter of split seconds between the fastest horse and the second- or third-place ones, you don't dare do anything to slow your horse. So she was always yelling at me, 'Keep your keister off the saddle!' So I did. And my times improved!"

"That is so cool!" I said.

"But do you know the best part?" Autumn Rose asked.

I shook my head no.

"My horse is happier than she used to be. She understands her job and she's enjoying it!"

I'm not sure what time it was when we fell asleep. I just know I dreamed about being a jockey that night. That very short night...

Mom knocked on my door way too early the next morning. It took me a few minutes to figure out what was going on. Finally, I realized she was using words like, 'Jeannie' and 'accident.' With that, I shot out of bed and opened my door.

Half a Saddle Off

Chapter 11
The Accident

"I'm sorry to wake you up so early, sweetheart, but Jeannie called. She's going to be okay, but she got hurt last night and needs you girls to help her. She asked me to feed you a big breakfast and send you over prepared to work all day.

Autumn Rose was conscious enough to understand too. We made record time getting our barn clothes on, snarfing down breakfast, picking up the lunches Mom had made for us, and heading out the door. Dad drove us to the barn, with none of the banter from last night.

We were worried.

Jeannie met us at the barn door, a little pale-looking, but actually smiling. "I went out on a date last night," she said. "Nice guy. Good dancer."

Autumn Rose and I looked at each other, confused. All this commotion because Jeannie went dancing?

She grimaced. "Unfortunately, it turns out that I'm not the dancer I thought I was. I kinda, sorta fell… and cracked my tailbone. The doctor said I'm not going to be on a horse for at least six weeks. That's really not good, since I just got in some new training horses."

I remembered her saying that she'd picked up some business from that last horse show.

"That's where you come in," Jeannie said. "You're going to be riding my training horses for me."

I felt my mouth drop open. I closed it again when no words came out.

"Autumn Rose, you're going to start on that filly I took to the horse show. Go brush her and put your saddle on her. I'll get her bridle and meet you at the round pen. And Meghan, you start cleaning stalls while I work with Autumn."

Feeling like a total loser, I turned away to find the pitchfork and wheelbarrow.

"Then you can swap off, Meghan," Jeannie said. "Autumn Rose can finish the barn chores while you work one of my others."

I took a breath, relieved. I *wasn't* a total loser! I wondered who Jeannie would put me on.

I was almost done with the last stall in the barn when I heard Jeannie. "Let Autumn Rose finish that, then she can start the outside pens. You go saddle up the stud colt."

Chapter 11 - The Accident

"I didn't think riders under the age of eighteen were allowed to ride stallions," I blurted out.

Jeannie said, "Well, you can't ride him in a show, but you can definitely ride this one under my supervision."

I left the wheelbarrow for Autumn Rose, then picked up the colt's halter. As I started toward his stall, Jeannie said, "Okay, the big difference for you, when handling a stud, is that you want his complete attention on you, one hundred percent of the time. If his focus isn't totally on you, get it there."

"How?" I asked.

"Depends on the situation. If you're leading him and his mind wanders off, snap the lead rope. With him, it shouldn't take more than that," she said.

I led him out of his stall, cross-tied him in the aisleway and went to work with the brushes, talking to him the whole time. Then I picked up the saddle blanket Jeannie told me was his, grabbed my saddle off the rack, and saddled him up. Jeannie ordered me to lead him to the round pen for some ground work.

As we walked out of the barn, Autumn Rose, having finished cooling the filly out, was leading her toward the barn. The colt looked in her direction.

"Meghan, snap him!" Jeannie commanded.

I gave a small jerk on the lead rope. He took his eyes off the filly and looked back to me.

"That's better," Jeannie said. "I've worked him hard on keeping his focus. Don't you dare let him lose that! A stud horse can be dangerous if you let his mind wander."

Once in the round pen, I took his halter off and free lunged him.

"I don't care whether you've got him trotting or loping; just keep him moving. And make him change directions often enough that he knows *you* are the one in charge."

After he had jogged, loped, and even bucked around the arena for a while, Jeannie said, "See how he's consistently keeping his inside ear cocked in your direction? That's excellent. He's focusing on you." A few minutes later, she said, "Do you see how he's starting to lick and chew? That means you're getting his brain engaged. That's just what you want, Meghan. You're doing a really nice job. I get the feeling you've done this sort of groundwork before."

"Yeah. My first horse was pretty opinionated. It took me a while to get her listening to me. There was a *lot* of groundwork in the process."

"Well, it's paying off today," Jeannie said. "At first, I wasn't sure if you'd be able to ride him right away. But I do believe you're going to get along just fine. You keep working him while I go get his bridle."

When I saw Jeannie coming back, I stopped, relaxed and stepped away from him, inviting him to walk up to me. He dropped back to a walk and came straight to me. In fact, he tried to come a little too close. I made a sudden jerky movement with my arms and he stopped abruptly.

Chapter 11 - The Accident

"Good job, Meghan," Jeannie said. "Never let a horse, especially a stud, walk into your personal space. You can walk into his, but he is *never* to walk into yours."

She hobbled into the round pen and handed me his bridle. "Watch that he doesn't get mouthy. Youngsters like him think nipping is fun."

Happily, he didn't try to bite. I think my unexpected arm movement made him leery of getting too close to me, which was a good thing. I put the bridle on without any difficulty, even though he raised his head a little.

"Your height is a real advantage when bridling," Jeannie remarked. "Now go ahead and step up on him. I want you to ride him in here until I see how you two get along."

I put my foot in the stirrup and swung up easily, landing like a feather, as Ol' Ben had taught me.

"Mounting is another place your height is handy," Jeannie said. "You make it look easy."

She stepped outside the gate, then asked me to walk him. I gathered up my reins, pushed lightly with my seat, and squeezed with both legs.

Nothing. He didn't move. I pushed and squeezed harder. He seemed to be thinking about moving but didn't actually do anything.

"Go ahead and bump him lightly with your legs this time," suggested Jeannie. "He's responding just right. I don't want him hurrying off from a standstill.

I like my horses to be real sure about what I want before they take the first step. They need to wait to see if I'm asking for a walk, a jog, a lope, a spin, a sidepass, or whatever. So his response was just perfect."

This time, as I pushed, squeezed, then bumped, he stepped out into a walk.

I quickly realized how light in the bridle he was being. It took only the slightest touch to get him to turn, collect, or stop.

After only a few loops around the pen, Jeannie said, "You two are a great match! Let's go out to the arena."

She opened the gate and I rode him through, ducking so as not to smack my helmet on the top bar. We turned and walked toward the main arena, with Jeannie chattering on about how she wished his owner had hands as soft as I do. That made me feel kinda proud.

Just then, one of the horses in an outside pen near the barn whinnied. The stud's head shot up and he whipped his head around toward the sound. Without actually thinking, I put him into a curl in the opposite direction. I wasn't mean about it, but I wasn't going to take no for an answer either.

His head dropped down and his focus snapped back to what I was asking.

"That mare you once owned must have made your life plenty interesting," Jeannie observed. "You've got some real good reactions."

While I rode the stud colt, Jeannie told me the owners' hopes for the horse, including being able to show him in

Versatility Ranch Horse contests. "So you just go ahead and ride him like you would Freckles, tuning him up for a reining class. That should be just what this boy needs. I'll sit back, um, make that *stand* back, and watch. I'll shout words of encouragement or correction if I need to. Otherwise, ride him like he's your own horse."

I looked over at Jeannie. She was clearly tired and in pain and, obviously, she couldn't sit down. I felt sorry for her and set about to work the colt as she wanted.

We started out with curls and counter-arcs at a walk, then jogged, loped, did drop-to-a-trot lead changes, and a few rollbacks. After about forty minutes, Jeannie said that was enough and that I should cool him out. While we walked around the arena, she asked, "Do you know where the term 'rollback' came from?"

"Um, no. I guess I don't."

"Back in the 1940s, a cowboy who worked on the King Ranch in Texas came up with the name. He was training cutting horses and decided there should be a name for the main maneuver they do. Since the horses turn 180 degrees, rolling back over their hind legs from one lead to the other when they turn cattle back, he coined the term rollback. And it stuck. He went on to help found the National Cutting Horse Association and was on the Board of Directors. His name was Monte Foreman. My father learned how to train horses from him."

"Cool," I said. Looking at Jeannie who was clearly exhausted. "My mentor in Colorado knew Monte Foreman too!"

"That's neat," she said, trying not to yawn. "Did you know that Monte also designed the original Western Riding class?"

"No, I didn't."

I walked the colt around the arena for another five minutes while she talked about horse-training history. "One of Monte's most prized possessions was a letter from the Spanish Riding School in Vienna, Austria, complimenting him on his work improving the way Western horses were being trained." She yawned again. "He really thought about things from the horse's point of view. That's what makes a good trainer."

More yawning.

"Okay. He's had enough walking. Dismount and walk him back to the barn. But keep his attention on you! Don't ever forget that," she said.

She walked with me and then waited for me to unsaddle the colt and put him back in his stall.

Autumn Rose came in as I finished and Jeannie said, "You girls ride your own horses. Then take a lunch break. I'll be back about 1:00 for the next round of training horses." With that she stumbled out of the barn and up to her house. We watched her the whole way, hoping she wouldn't pass out and keel over.

"Wow. She's hurting," Autumn Rose said.

"Yeah."

Chapter 11 - The Accident

Autumn Rose surprised me by saying she wanted to do some jumping. And I surprised myself by saying I thought that sounded like fun. That's apparently what Jeannie had been planning for us too, because she had put the jumps out in the arena after we had left yesterday, no doubt before she had gone dancing. The jumps were set up about nine to ten feet apart, as a no-stride, so that our horses would hop through like deer.

After the warm-up, I explained it to Autumn Rose as best as I could remember: "This is a triple, no-stride in-and-out. The horses are going to go through it like a deer bouncing away from a predator. But the jumps are set really low so it'll be fun, not scary. I promise! All you have to do is stand up in two-point the whole way through, keeping your eyes up, your heels down, and your horse going straight. Nothing to it! Watch."

I cantered Freckles to it and he bounced on through.

"Now you try it," I told her.

She cantered Sage up to the in-and-out while I called out reminders. "Keep your eyes up. Stand up from the stride before you get to the first jump to a stride after the last one. And keep your heels down!"

After she made several good passes through it, we raised each jump a hole, about three inches, and she came through twice more. Then I took Freckles through at that height. We raised them another hole and I took him through again. Surprisingly, Autumn Rose wanted to try that height too. Then Freckles and I went another hole higher. Autumn Rose dropped out at that height. But then she raised them yet another hole for us.

"You two look like you're having the best time ever!"

"That's only because we are!" I agreed.

I wanted to go higher still, but I was afraid it would be too hard on Freckles' legs. Jumping is a lot of work.

Autumn Rose must have been thinking the same way. "We should probably go cool the horses out," she said.

We walked out around our usual loop along the irrigation canals. As we passed Sadie's, I said, "I think they're gone to the High School State Finals Rodeo this weekend."

"I don't know anything about their travels. Sadie hasn't talked to me since the horse show," Autumn Rose said quietly.

"Oh, don't feel too special. She hasn't talked to me since then either," I said.

When Autumn Rose spoke again, I was a little surprised to hear her say, "I truly do feel sorry for Sadie."

"Seriously?"

"Yeah. Either she never listened to the wisdom of her elders or she was never taught. I don't know which. But she is misguided," Autumn Rose said.

"How do you mean?" I asked.

"She loves *things*. And she *uses* animals and people. That is not the way to happiness. She needs to learn to love animals and people, and to use things."

"That's a really good way to look at—well—things," I said.

"It's just simple truth, if you think about it," she told me.

We rode in companionable silence back to the barn, took care of our horses, and had just enough time for lunch before Jeannie hobbled back to the barn.

"This time you're going to take turns doing some groundwork in the round pen; then you'll ride together in the big arena. Autumn Rose, you're going to ride Grover. He's a 14-year-old gelding that belongs to an 11-year-old girl who wants to 'do everything,' according to her mother. You'll be working on tuning up the horse's responses and improving his movement. I want you to ride him with your Western saddle today, but use one of my D-ring snaffles with the long split reins. You're going to have to take him back to basics and work through some bad habits."

Autumn Rose picked up a halter and went to find the horse.

"Meghan, you're going to be working on the same things as Autumn Rose, but you'll be riding a spoiled mare that belongs to an older woman. You probably saw her at the show. The mare never did anything particularly awful. She just did what *she* wanted instead of what the rider asked. So same thing: put on your Western saddle and a training bridle with a D-ring and some long split reins."

Since Autumn Rose had a head start, she got to the round pen ahead of me and was doing her groundwork by the time I finished saddling. Her training horse was a cute little red roan. I was glad Jeannie hadn't assigned me to ride him. I'd have had to jack up my stirrups like a jockey to keep my feet from dragging on the ground.

Not that my horse was big. She was a good three inches shorter than Freckles, but at least I wasn't going to have to change my stirrups more than one hole. Color-wise she was a nondescript sorrel without a speck of white anywhere on her body. I led her over to the round pen and watched.

After Autumn Rose finished, we started our groundwork. At first, the mare wasn't paying any attention to me and I practically had to jump in front of her to make her turn around. But eventually, I was able to stay in the middle of the round pen and turn her with just my body language.

When Jeannie was satisfied with our progress, she told me to put the bridle on the mare and lead her to the arena.

"What's her name?" I asked Jeannie.

She had to think about it for a minute. "Roxy."

"Okay, Roxy, let's go have some fun," I told the mare.

"The first thing I want you both to do is to make sure the horse stands still while you mount up," Jeannie said. "If they don't stand rock still, correct them immediately, then dismount and mount again, until they do."

Chapter 11 - The Accident

Autumn Rose's horse was standing quietly by the second try. With Roxy, I had to dismount and mount back up at least eight times, before she would stand.

Jeannie had us both work the horses at a walk, jog, and lope, doing circles and reverses, working to make them softer with our aids. Ol' Ben used to tell me to "ask" the horse nicely for what I wanted, then "tell", then "make." And of course, the minute the horse did what I wanted, he would tell me to reward the horse.

Jeannie told us the same thing, but she used different words.

"Just suggest what you want your horse to do. If you get what you want, leave the horse alone. That's *really* important! If you don't get what you want, get a little more insistent with your aids, so the horse understands you mean business. If the horse still doesn't give you what you want, kill him."

She said that very matter-of-factly. Autumn Rose looked as surprised as I felt. Jeannie must've noticed.

"Well, not literally, of course. Don't really kill him. That makes clients unhappy. But definitely let the horse know you mean business. And don't be nice about it. I mean, you have to be fair and make the punishment fit the crime, so the horse understands what he's supposed to do. But you may have to get tough to make him behave."

"How do we do that?" I asked. "This mare really doesn't want to go forward. When I put my legs on her and push her with my seat, she just sort of ignores me. How do you want me to, um, kill her?"

"Those long, split reins you've got," Jeannie said. "You're going to over-and-under her if she ignores both your initial suggestion and then your second request."

"What do you mean? Over-and-under?" I asked.

Jeannie pretended she was holding both reins in one hand, then used her other hand to grab the long ends and swing them from one side to the other and back again, as if she were hitting her imaginary horse on its rump with her imaginary reins.

I could see what she meant. So the next time Roxy ignored my legs, I grabbed the ends of the reins and swung them the way she had showed us. Unfortunately, however, I swung them too high, missing the horse completely and swatting myself in the back.

Jeannie, once she had stopped laughing, suggested, "You need to aim a little lower."

Once again, I asked with my legs (and was ignored,) told with my legs (only to be ignored again,) then kicked a third time while doing the over-and-under. My aim was much better and I swatted the mare four times in a row, twice on each side. She jumped forward into a lope, as I had initially asked.

Her lope was way too fast though, so I tried to slow her down.

"No!" Jeannie shouted. "Let her run. You told her to run, so let her. Don't confuse her by pulling her back when she finally agreed to go forward!"

I let her run. Slowly she slowed down to a reasonable speed and loped nicely halfway around the arena.

Chapter 11 - The Accident

"Bring her back to a walk," Jeannie told me. "Let her air up for a few minutes, then suggest that she lope again. This isn't a very ambitious horse. So as soon as she figures out she's going to have to do what you want, I think she will quickly learn how to do it with the least amount of effort."

The mare couldn't be bothered to lope when I asked, but by the second kick, her head came up and her ears flicked back as if she were at least thinking about it. By the third kick, I over-and-undered her again. She jumped out into a fast lope, as she had done the previous time, but this time I didn't try to slow her down. She soon slowed down on her own.

"Try it again," Jeannie said.

I suggested with my legs and weight that she should canter, then I started to use my legs a little harder. She stepped out into a lope before I had to over-and-under her.

"Well done!" Jeannie said. After we'd gone halfway around the arena, Jeannie said, "Now stop her and let her rest and think about what she just learned."

Jeannie worked with Autumn Rose on her training horse's transitions from one gait to the other for a while, then told me to get out on the rail and work my mare a little more. This time the mare was listening to my legs much better. When I asked her to lope, she did on the first suggestion. I was really proud of her.

"Go walk these two out. They've had enough for today. When you get back, you each have one more horse to ride," Jeannie said. "I'm going up to the house for a few minutes."

As we walked out toward the irrigation canal, Autumn Rose said, "This is really cool, getting to ride all these horses!"

"Yeah, it is! I mean, I'm sorry that Jeannie got hurt, but wow! This is fun!"

By the time we got back to the barn, Jeannie was hobbling back toward us. "Get them unsaddled; then you go get Vincent, Autumn Rose. I've been riding him for about a month and he's a sweetheart. Meghan, you get that new horse that came in yesterday. The owner said she's pretty mellow. She just needs us to get the mare legged up and tuned up."

Autumn Rose only did a few minutes of ground-work; just enough to get Vincent to join up with her. I had to spend a little more time at it because the mare, Angel, was new to it. She could probably have used more time in the round pen, but Jeannie was obviously getting tired. She told us to take the horses to the big arena and mount up.

We walked them around the arena each direction, then eased both horses out into a jog. After only one time around, Angel stopped, as if to say she'd had enough and was done now. I sat back and suggested she resume jogging. She pinned her ears back and refused to budge. As I started to kick a little harder, the mare's head and neck disappeared between her front legs and she started bucking.

My reins had been loose, encouraging her to go forward. I began frantically trying to get my reins gathered up as she bucked across the arena. I was able to get her head up at last and bend it around to my kneecap so she couldn't buck effectively anymore. The minute I had her head, I started kicking her with my legs and over-and-undering her too. Once she was trying to get away from my legs, I let her head go straight and she trotted forward fast.

We trotted halfway around the arena before I became aware of Jeannie's voice shouting my name.

"Meghan, stop her! Meghan! Meghan, let the mare stop!"

I eased back on the reins and said, "Whoa." Slowly, she came back to me.

Jeannie walked over to me. "Are you okay?"

"Yeah, I'm fine. Why?" I asked.

Autumn Rose started laughing.

Jeannie did *not* laugh. "Because I didn't expect that behavior from this mare. I suspected she was a little spoiled, but not to the extent that she is! I saved her for last today because I thought she would be your easy ride."

This time I laughed.

Jeannie was still serious though. "You don't have to ride this mare, Meghan. I can send her home and tell them I can't work with her 'til this fall. Or they can send her to another trainer."

"Why? Did I handle her wrong? How was I supposed to do it?" I asked, concerned.

"No, are you kidding me? I was impressed that you were still on top when the dust settled, and that you actually had her doing what you had asked for in the first place," Jeannie said.

"Well, to be honest, she's not much more difficult than my first horse was," I said. "Someone gave her to me for free, and that little Palomino mare stuck my head in the dirt regularly in the first few weeks I had her."

"Wow, I'm surprised you're still riding if your first horse was like this," said Autumn Rose.

"Yeah, she bucked me off a bunch of times before we worked out our issues," I said.

"Well this mare didn't even come close to bucking you off," Jeannie said. "You stuck to her like velcro!"

I hadn't really thought about it. "Yeah. I guess I did." This horse had bucked longer and harder than my mare ever had. Yet, she hadn't gotten me off her back. I was kinda proud of that.

"It's all that jumping you've been doing. You're learning how to go with the horse when it leaves the ground," Jeannie said.

"I definitely like it better up here," I said.

"Yeah!" Jeannie agreed. "But the question remains, do you want me to send this horse home? Seriously, you do *not* have to keep riding her."

"I'm not scared, if that's what you're asking. I know what to expect now, and I'll try not to let her catch me off-guard like she did this time. So, if you're willing to keep her here, I want to keep riding her," I said.

We worked the horses for another forty-five minutes, then took them for their cool-out walk.

Jeannie met us back at the barn when we returned. "Will you girls please help me feed once you've got your horses put up?" she asked. Her voice sounded different when she spoke, and I noticed that her walk was even more wobbly.

We put the horses away and hurried back into the barn. Jeannie told us to go load hay in the wheelbarrows and throw hay to each of the horses while she refilled their water buckets. Then we met her back at the feed room, where she was starting to measure out cans of feed and supplements.

"Jeannie," I said as we waited for her to fill the first few cans, "we were wondering if you wanted us to get Sadie to come help ride the horses. She should be home Monday and—"

"No! Not a chance," Jeannie said abruptly. "She wouldn't know what to do on a horse that her parents hadn't paid a small fortune for. That's the only kind she can ride. I need riders who can train horses, not ruin them."

I was surprised into silence by that.

"Here." She shoved a can of feed at me and ordered, "Take this one to the stud colt," then handing me a second one said, "and this one to Roxy." She handed two more to Autumn Rose, telling her which cans went to which horses.

The process continued like that, although once she told Autumn to take the grain to "Victor." We didn't have a Victor on the place, or at least, not one that either of us knew about.

"Victor?" Autumn Rose asked. "Which pen is he in?"

Jeannie sounded annoyed. "You rode him today; you should know where you put him away."

"Oh, I thought his name was Vincent," Autumn Rose said uncertainly.

"Victor. Vincent. Whatever. Just give him his grain," Jeannie said.

By the time we were finished, Jeannie was slurring her words so badly we were having trouble understanding her. She was really unsteady on her feet too.

"Jeannie, I'd like to walk back to the house with you," I said.

"Whatever," she said in an oddly garbled voice.

Over my shoulder, I mouthed the words, "Go get your mom!"

Autumn Rose took off for their trailer. By the time Jeannie and I got as far as the house, Autumn Rose and her mother were waiting beside Jeannie's door.

"What's this? A party?" Jeannie said. At least, I think that's what she said.

"Yes, it is," Autumn Rose's mom said cheerily "Let's go inside and talk."

Chapter 11 - The Accident

By now, Jeannie was leaning heavily against me, so I helped her into her house and toward the nearest chair. A wooden one.

"I can't park my busted butt on that hard ol' thing," Jeannie said. "I want something soft and comfy."

We continued into the living room to a big cushy sofa. Even so, as she sat down, Jeannie was clearly uncomfortable, so she just sort of keeled over onto her side. I pulled her boots off and helped her put her feet up too.

Autumn Rose's mom followed us from the kitchen, where she had stopped and picked up a couple of things. "Are these your pain pills?" she asked.

Jeannie said, "Yup."

"And did you wash them down with this?" She held up a bottle of wine.

"Sure did," she said. "I was kinda shook up watching Shorty here ride that spoiled bronc. I needed something to calm my nerves."

"Jeannie," Autumn's mom said kindly, "you can't drink alcohol when you're on pain meds like this."

"Is that right?" she mumbled and drifted off to sleep.

"Meghan, you girls did the right thing, bringing her back to the house and calling me over."

"Is she going to be okay?" I asked.

"It doesn't look as if she had very much to drink, so I think she'll be all right. But I'm going to sit with her until I'm certain. You can go on home, Meghan. Autumn Rose will help me if I need anything."

"If you're sure..." I said, feeling relieved but also slightly guilty to be bailing out on them.

"I'm sure. Besides, this will give my daughter and me time to catch up. I want to hear all about your sleepover."

I left the two of them chatting away while Jeannie slept.

The sleepover. That seemed so far away. But it was only last night.

Time is weird.

Chapter 12
Meet the Bull

The next morning, I biked out to the ranch early to help feed. Jeannie seemed back to normal, a little pale and clearly still in pain, but at least she was talking normally. And she was embarrassed.

"I'm so sorry for my behavior yesterday," she said. "I should have known not to drink wine when I'm taking pain pills. That was stunningly stupid! But I was so upset when I saw Angel start bucking with you, Meghan. I was terrified that you were going to get hurt because I had put you on a horse that I knew almost nothing about."

"It's okay, Jeannie. I didn't get hurt."

"No, but you could have. All because of me."

"Jeannie, if it makes you feel any better, Autumn Rose and I were talking while we were cooling out Vincent and Roxy, and except for the fact that you were hurt, we agreed we were having the best day ever, getting to ride all those horses! We both learned a ton!"

"We're really grateful for the opportunity," Autumn Rose chimed in. "And we're hoping you'll let us continue."

"Of course I will, if you're sure," Jeannie said.

"I'm sure!" Autumn Rose and I both said at exactly the same moment.

"Okay. But one more thing. You have to promise never to repeat what I said about Sadie! Not to anyone!" she pleaded.

"Of course we won't say anything," I said.

"We'd never intentionally hurt her feelings like that," Autumn Rose added.

The next month flew by as Autumn Rose and I continued to ride our own horses, plus "our" training horses, while Jeannie coached us on what we needed to do. The horses' owners had all agreed to allow us to continue, which made both of us feel pretty good.

I was having a blast on the stud colt, working on developing his turn-arounds (spins), his flying lead changes, and his stops. And the two mares, Roxy and Angel, had quit acting like sullen brats and were turning into willing partners. I hadn't had to resort to the over-and-under technique since the second day on Roxy and the fourth day on Angel. Both had now accepted the fact that I was their leader. They were listening to me better each day, responding to my suggestions, my *asking*, right away, not wanting me to have to *tell* them to do anything a second time. That made life a lot easier for them and for me!

Chapter 12 - Meet the Bull

Autumn Rose was having a great time on her horses also. It was fun watching their progress! Her confidence in jumping was soaring too, as she had thrown herself wholeheartedly into practicing.

Late one afternoon, while cooling out our last set of horses, Autumn Rose asked, "Are you planning to go to the dance Saturday night?"

"Uh…is this a trick question?" I asked. "Because A: I don't know anything about a dance Saturday night, and B: I barely know how to dance, since I've never actually gone to one before."

"Oh, I thought you'd have heard about it. One of the high school groups is putting it on this weekend at the fairgrounds community hall."

"Nope. Haven't heard a thing," I said. "Or if I did, it didn't impress any of my brain cells enough that any of 'em bothered to remember it."

"Well, now that you know, would you consider going?" she asked. "I don't want to be there without knowing anyone else in the place."

"I'll have to ask my parents," I said, uncertainly.

As we approached Sadie's, I noticed an unusually large number of people gathered around out by the lean-to where the mechanical bull was kept.

"I wonder what's going on?" I said, not expecting a response.

Autumn Rose surprised me by answering. "They finally got a bull riding coach."

"How did you find that out?" I asked in surprise. "Have you been talking to Sadie?"

"Hardly," she laughed, "since she never comes for lessons anymore."

Just then, a familiar voice called from near the mechanical bull. "Autumn Rose! Hand your horse to your friend and come over here."

It took me a few seconds to figure out whose voice it was. Finally, as she handed me her reins, I realized it was her father's.

Autumn Rose climbed over the fence, crossed the arena, and went through the gate to where the crowd was gathered. They parted to let her walk through to where her Dad was standing.

I couldn't hear clearly, but I *thought* I heard her father say, "Climb up on this bull."

Suddenly, things got really quiet.

Once Autumn Rose was on top of the bull, I could see her head and shoulders above the crowd. She appeared to grab the bull rope, fiddling with it for several seconds to get a proper hold. Then she sat back and nodded.

The bull lurched into motion, bucking and spinning.

Autumn Rose stayed on, riding it a full eight seconds!

After they shut the machine off, she jumped down and I lost her in the crowd again. But a few minutes later, she came jogging across the arena and climbed the fence. As she got close, she smiled up at me and said, "Your turn."

"You're kidding," I said in disbelief.

"No. I'm not. Dad wants you to go try it," she said. "It's actually kinda fun! Just listen to his instructions. Especially when he tells you to lean back on that first jump. Otherwise, you *are* going to come off over the front."

I sat there, staring down at her.

"Meghan. Get over there. They're all waiting for you."

I dismounted and made the trek across the arena, wondering if I were being a total idiot—being fairly certain that I was.

I walked through the crowd, recognizing the regular high school rodeo boys. The rest appeared to be girlfriends, parents, and siblings of the boys. I towered over most of them. I saw Lane smirking at me out of the corner of my eye. Sadie, who was just beyond him, looked a little worried.

Autumn's dad asked, "Meghan, have you ever ridden a bull or a mechanical bull before?"

"No, sir," I responded.

"Are you willing to give it a try?"

"Yes, sir, as long as you tell me what to do," I said, climbing up onto the platform.

As I settled onto the bull's plastic back, Autumn's dad showed me how to take a proper hold on the bull rope for the best grip. "Keep your knees bent, so you can lift yourself off his back," he said. "If you try to just sit on his back, you can be bucked off. Keep your shoulders square, but be flexible. Tuck your chin a little bit. Move straight forward and straight back, but not too much, just a little bit, just like riding a horse. You need to dance with him, not fight with him. And don't try to lean with the bull's turns; just stay straight. If you're leaning one direction, a smart bull will jump back the other way and leave you hangin' out to the side with nothin' under you but dirt."

He turned toward the onlookers. "This girl has a helmet on, just like my daughter did. That's 'cause these girls are smart, and they both intend to stay that way. The brain is pretty soft and mushy. It needs something to protect it if—*when*—you come off on your head. And listen up, cowboys: as hard-headed as some of you boys are, you can't protect your brain with just your skull. You need to be wearing a helmet."

Turning back to me, he said, "Okay, Meghan, it's just like jumping a horse; you get off his back and let him jump; as soon as he crests, get underneath your rope."

"I'm not sure I understand what that means," I said uncertainly.

"When he 'crests' means that he's reached the highest part of his upward jump. Then he begins to come back down, getting ready to kick his hind legs out," he explained.

"Um, what about the 'get underneath your rope' part?" I asked.

"Just kinda lean your upper body back a slight amount while keeping your legs clamped around his barrel, just behind his shoulders. Does that make sense?"

"Yes, sir," I answered, trying to visualize the proper position in my head and imagine what it would feel like.

"Oh, and when the bull rises up in the jump, push your arm into the bull's shoulders."

He gave me another minute to think about what he'd just told me, then finally asked, "Are you ready?"

I nodded my head, forgetting that's the signal for the operator to start the action.

The bull's hind end pitched up hard, throwing me forward. Fortunately, because of Autumn Rose's example and her dad's advice, I had been leaning back far enough that I was able to fight gravity and stay on. The bull pitched and spun and changed direction without warning. But I focused and, somehow, I stuck with it.

After what seemed like eight minutes, the eight second whistle blew and the operator shut down the bull.

"Nice job, Meghan. Now, tell me, have you ever tried to ride any kind of bucking bull before?" Mr. Ifaita asked again.

"No, sir."

I threw my leg over the bull and slid down. Making eye contact with Lane, I said, "But it was almost as fun as riding a jumping horse." I walked back through the crowd, trying to keep my shaky legs going in a straight line.

Mr. Ifaita continued his instruction, "You boys need to ride bareback as much as you can on a horse. You need to ride in a round pen and lunge over small jumps until you're able to be a part of the horse's motion. It's a lot easier to learn the basics on horseback."

I heard one of the boys say, "I'm not some wussy English rider!" To my surprise, it wasn't Lane's voice.

However, the next voice *was* Lane's. "In two months of practicing, Clay, you haven't stayed on a bull yet. But both of those *English* riders just did. So maybe you ought to reconsider."

When the laughter subsided, Autumn Rose's dad continued. "We're going to hang up a bucking barrel for practice too. Using just a bucking machine can ruin a bull rider because only about two percent of the bulls have the suckback when they buck and can cause the rider to go into the horns. A bucking barrel will give you more opportunity to practice, which you all need because you have to learn not to overthink, just react. Another thing: You've also got to exercise: do lots of stretches, core exercises. Don't try to bulk up with weights though. That takes away from your oxygen intake. Stay as flexible as possible; run three miles a day; eat healthy; and drink lots of water!"

His voice faded as I approached Autumn Rose. As I took my reins back from her, she deadpanned, "Did I mention that Dad is the new bull riding coach?"

"Is that right?" I said, playing along. "Do tell."

"Well, yes. Apparently someone found out that he has won or been in the Top Ten at the Indian National Finals Rodeo for most all of the past fifteen years," she said. "Even so, some of the members weren't sure they wanted him for a coach. I guess they thought bulls bucked differently at our rodeos than they do at theirs."

"You have got to be kidding me."

"Afraid not," she said.

"Why are people so stupid sometimes?" I wondered aloud.

Autumn Rose just shrugged her shoulders. No one could answer that question.

"Well, now we've given them something new to be miffed about. They can complain that he's good at coaching *girls*." I giggled. " 'Cause he is!"

"I truly do hope they'll cut him some slack after seeing *we* could ride after following his advice," Autumn Rose said.

"So how did he know we'd be able to do it?" I asked.

"Well, he's coached me on bucking barrels when I was a kid. I could stay on pretty well. I guess he figured I could probably handle this too," she said.

"But why did he think I could?"

"He's watched you ride," Autumn Rose said. "In fact, he saw one of Angel's bucking episodes, and he was impressed at how well you handled it."

"Oh! Cool!"

"Besides, he says the jumping we do has taught us a lot about how to ride a bucker," she said. "He definitely sees the value of learning to ride English."

"Know something? I think I do too!"

⁓

While we warmed up our first set of training horses the next morning, Autumn Rose said, "My father asked me to thank you. He said that after you and I rode, he was able to make some headway with the boys. Most of them actually started listening to him. He said that all but two of the boys showed some real improvement."

"Oh wow! Those two must've got ragged unmercifully by the other bull riders." I could just imagine it.

"Yeah," Autumn Rose said. "Dad had to put a stop to that. And fortunately, by then they had decided he was worthy of their respect, so he *was* able to back them off."

"Cool!"

"Dad said he will be coaching the boys twice a week for the next few months." She smiled slyly. "He said we can come over and ride with them whenever we want."

"Yeah…No! I don't think I need to pursue bull riding as a hobby. But please, thank him for his kind and generous offer," I giggled.

"Did you ask your parents if you could go to the dance?" she asked.

"Actually, I did."

"Well, what'd they say?"

"I figured you'd know the answer, since your parents had already called mine to ask them to let me go along." I hesitated. "What's up with that?"

"Umm...they're helping chaperone the dance," she responded.

"How'd they get roped into that?" I asked.

"Good choice of words, 'roped,'" she laughed. "The high school rodeo team is sponsoring the team roping event at the fairgrounds this weekend. They decided to include a dance Saturday night, and as a team coach, Dad volunteered to be a chaperone."

"Ah…" I said.

"So? What did your parents say? Can you come too?" Autumn Rose persisted.

"Well, yeah, I can. I'm just not sure I want to."

Autumn Rose looked so bummed that I immediately felt bad for what I'd just said.

"I don't know if going to a dance with a bunch of rodeo team people who don't like me sounds like that much fun," I added.

"Why would you think they don't like you?" she asked.

"Are you kidding? They've made that clear all summer!"

Autumn Rose got real quiet, and we both went back to working our horses. It wasn't until we had both stopped again to let our horses air up that she spoke again.

"Did you like riding English at first?" she asked.

"You know I didn't."

"What changed your mind?"

"Because it's actually fun. And it improved my riding."

"So, if *you* changed your mind about it, don't you think it's possible that they may have had a change of heart about it too? Especially after we showed them the value of it when it comes to *their* sport?"

"Well, maybe. I guess."

"Then come to the dance. You've shown them you're not a wussy English rider. Now show them you're not a snooty one who's unwilling to hang out with them," she said.

This time, I got quiet. I started working my horse again, and Autumn Rose did the same. When I finally stopped my horse for air-up time, she stopped her horse beside me. She looked at me, clearly expecting an answer.

Chapter 12 - Meet the Bull

"Okay," I said. "I'll come."

She smiled. "Thanks."

Jeannie finally showed up at the arena. "I've been watching you girls from the house. You did a great job with these horses this morning! Every time I wished I was within yelling distance to tell you to do something, it was as if you were reading my mind and you did it! You've both really developed a sense of what your horses need."

I didn't know what to say and just mumbled a quiet, "Thanks."

Autumn Rose said it better. "We couldn't have done this without you. You've taught us a lot, and you've given us a great opportunity."

"You both have given me a lot too. In fact, after your antics last evening, my phone has been ringing practically non-stop with bull riders wanting riding lessons." She added, "I wish I'd have been there to see it! I can't believe you two! What a crazy stunt!"

Jeannie's phone rang. "Go work these two horses on the sidepassing we started with them yesterday," she said as she walked away to take the call.

I wasn't trying to listen to her call, but I couldn't help hearing her ask, "How bad is it?"

Briefly, I wondered if her ex-husband was causing problems again. If that were the case, I knew I needed to get busy working my horse so I didn't give her someone to vent her anger on when she hung up the phone.

I asked the mare to do a turn-on-the-forehand each direction to remind her she should move her hip away from my leg when I laid it back behind the girth. Once I knew she was listening to my legs, I moved her shoulders sideways with my hands and her hip sideways with my leg, getting her to sidepass a couple of steps. She understood and moved over willingly, so I let her stop to think for a minute before asking her to do it the other direction. She was good that way too, so I let her stop again.

"Autumn Rose! Meghan!" Jeannie called as she put her phone back in her pocket. "Come over here."

As we walked back to where she stood, Autumn Rose and I glanced at each other. Autumn Rose looked a little worried too.

"I truly hate to tell you this, but you need to know: Sadie tried to ride the bull after everyone left last night. She didn't get it done."

"Oh no! Is she all right?" I asked.

"Well, not completely. She hit her head and she wasn't wearing a helmet. They kept her overnight in the hospital for observation. I'll let you know when I hear more."

It wasn't until late afternoon that we saw Sadie's Mom drive slowly up their driveway. She stopped close to their front door, then came around to the passenger side and helped Sadie out of the car. We both waved, and Sadie raised her hand in a sort of wave back before disappearing into the house.

Chapter 12 - Meet the Bull

After we put our horses up and finished our chores, Autumn Rose and I walked over to Sadie's house.

Mrs. Hardin—Angie—met us at the door. "Sadie's sleeping," she said. "She's going to have to take it easy for a few days. Maybe you girls could stop by tomorrow. I'm sure she'd love to see you."

⁓

"Mom said we should take Sadie some flowers. I don't get why flowers are supposed to make someone feel better, but that's apparently how it's done. Anyway, instead of a bouquet, which would just wilt and die in a few days, I talked Mom into this." I held up a small pot with a miniature rosebush in it.

"Pink roses. That's perfect," observed Autumn Rose. "I made her a card."

She held up a large sheet of paper that she'd folded in half. On the front she had drawn a picture of Sadie riding Deluxe. Inside it read, "Hope you're back in the saddle again soon."

"Wow! You're a good artist!"

Autumn Rose blushed, but looked pleased that I thought so.

Sadie's mom opened the door when we knocked and ushered us into the house. Sadie was lying on the living room couch. She looked tired and a little pale.

"I'll leave you girls to talk," Sadie's mother said.

We gave Sadie the plant and her card. She looked at them, then looked at us. "Well aren't you going to say it?"

"Say what?" I asked.

"Aren't you going to ask how I could've done something so stupid? That's the first thing everyone else has said." Her voice trailed off.

"No. I was going to ask if you're going to be able to come to the dance Saturday night," Autumn Rose said.

"Yeah, and I want to know how we're supposed to dress for this thing. Are cowboy boots okay for dancing in?" I asked, trying to sound as if I were serious.

It worked. Sadie actually smiled.

"Yes. Cowboy boots are perfect," she said to me. Then turning to Autumn Rose, she continued, "And I'm hoping to go! Mom's making me do three days of 'bed rest,' or 'house arrest,' as Lane calls it. But that ends on Friday. Mom says if I take it easy 'til then, I should be able to go."

"Great!" we said in stereo.

But then no one seemed to know what to say, and the silence grew uncomfortably long.

"I am so sorry for what I said the last time I talked to you, Meghan," Sadie finally blurted out. "And Autumn Rose, I was pretty rude to you, too, even though I don't think I actually said anything out loud. Anyhow, I am so sorry," she repeated.

"We all have bad days, Sadie. What I said to you in the tack room, about still thinking I'm your friend, has never changed," I told her. "I've been hoping all along that you'd start feeling that way again too. So—apology accepted!"

"Sadie, I will *always* go out to win. If you can accept that, I will enjoy our friendship very much," Autumn Rose said. "Even when *you* beat me."

"You mean *if* I beat you. You're really good. And I didn't expect that," Sadie admitted.

"But you'll keep practicing and you'll keep learning, and so will I, because competing against each other will make us both want to improve," Autumn Rose said.

"I guess I'm gonna have to learn to ride English now, too, since you guys have made it a cool thing to do," Sadie said. "Even Lane wants to learn after seeing you two ride the bull."

"Look at us!" I poked at Autumn Rose. "We're trendsetters."

"Yeah, well that's why I had to try to ride the bull," Sadie said. "After everyone left, I was mad at myself that you had ridden it, and I hadn't even tried."

"Who was helping you?" I asked.

"No one!" Sadie said, quickly and loudly. "I was by myself."

"How does that work?" I asked. "How do you reach the start button when you're sitting on the bull?"

Sadie's eyes darted toward the kitchen, where her mother had gone. Loudly she said, "Oh, it has a remote start feature. I was able to start it through my phone."

"Oh," I said.

Another uncomfortable silence started.

Autumn Rose finally said, "We've got more chores to do. We better be getting back."

"Okay. Thanks for coming to see me," Sadie said.

"Yeah, see you at the dance," I said.

"Well, that got awkward," I said when we were out of earshot of the house.

Autumn Rose nodded her head in agreement, then asked, "Why do you think she lied to us?"

"Yeah, it was weird. Especially since it was only, like, two seconds after she apologized for her, um, unpleasantness after the horse show. She sounded as if she meant the apology, but then to turn around and lie to us in the next breath…"

Autumn Rose said, "I wonder who she's trying to protect?"

"You mean, who was with her and actually ran the controls for the bucking bull?" I asked.

Chapter 13
The Dance

I wanted to go watch some of the team roping on Saturday, but a few of Jeannie's clients were coming out that day, and she needed me to ride two of the horses so the owners could see how well they were doing. One woman got so emotional seeing her horse, Angel, all calm and relaxed, that she started to cry tears of joy. Jeannie asked her if she'd like to take a lesson on Angel, and she got practically giddy.

I stepped down and shortened the stirrups for her. She mounted up nervously. But soon she was petting the mare and hugging her around the neck, telling her how proud she was of Angel for having magically transformed into such a nice horse.

Jeannie assured her that there was no magic involved—just a lot of wet saddle blankets.

Later, Angel's owner brushed the mare after I pulled my saddle off her and lugged it back to the tack room.

"Do you use a spray bottle or a hose to make the saddle blanket wet?" Angel's owner asked Jeannie. "Or do you just dunk it in a bucket? What's the easiest way? I'm so proud of Angel. I don't want her to lose any of the magic you've worked on her."

I took one look at Jeannie's face and had to turn around and walk out of the barn to keep from exploding with laughter. Somehow, Jeannie patiently explained to the woman, again, that there had been no magic involved in her mare's transformation. "The wet saddle blankets I was referring to were from sweat, not water. It took a lot of hours of good training from a knowledgeable horse person to make these changes in your mare. The only way you're going to keep your mare behaving well is to ride Angel in lessons, so you can learn how to communicate with her the way Meghan does. If you'll do that, you can become a good partner with your mare."

"A partner?" the woman asked.

"Yes. Riding is a lot like dancing. You need to be a good leader for your horse, so she understands what you're asking for and can read your slightest cues," Jeannie said. "You need to learn to read her body language as well. If you'll put in the time and effort it takes to learn how to do that, you two will develop a good partnership."

While they were still talking, I finished my chores, cuddled Threepio, then waved goodbye to Jeannie, who was still trying to explain things to her client.

Chapter 13 - The Dance

Jeannie called out, "You be careful at that dance tonight. I can't afford to have you injured!"

I promised her I would, then biked home to get ready.

⁓

Mom dropped me off at the fairgrounds a few hours later, hours I spent showering, trying to get my hair under control, applying make-up, and picking out my nicest jeans and most feminine top. It was kinda fun trying to look my best for a change.

As I got out of the car, I was surprised to see Autumn Rose walking toward the building. "Whoa, wait! I thought you were coming to the dance with your parents, Autumn Rose."

She turned around and saw me. "They already went in. But I spent a few extra minutes at our truck after we got here. My hair isn't being very cooperative tonight," she said. "Does it look okay now?"

All I could see was a gorgeous, beaded barrette from which her hair fell in beautiful, black waves down past her belt.

"Oh my gosh, it looks fabulous! And that barrette is a work of art!"

She blushed slightly as she admitted, "I made it."

"Are you kidding? That's a gorgeous piece!" I put my hands on my hips and tried to look annoyed. "Barrels, dressage, artwork, beading... Is there anything you can't do?" I demanded.

"Yes," she said. "I can't reach things on high shelves. That's why I decided to befriend you."

"Oh well, good to know I've got one talent anyway."

Autumn Rose's voice dropped as she asked, "Are you as nervous as I am?"

"Oh yeah. The butterflies are having their own dance party in my stomach right now. So," I asked, turning around as if I were a model, "how do I look?"

"Tall and gorgeous," she said.

"Well, okay then. Since we're agreed that we are both lookin' good, let's get inside and dazzle everyone," I said, lifting my ribcage and stretching to my full height. "We can do this."

We started up the walkway toward the door.

As I reached for the handle, I heard a familiar voice from around the corner of the building. "Watch this! Watch this! Here's where she gets launched!"

A different voice exclaimed, "Oh, man, she really caught some air!"

A third voice said, "Whoa, she landed hard. Is she okay?"

Autumn Rose and I both stopped and looked at each other.

The familiar voice said, "Yeah, she's fine. She had to take it easy for a few days, but she's okay now. She oughta be here any minute. You guys can meet her. She's seriously hot! But don't go getting' any ideas. This one's mine."

Chapter 13 - The Dance

That's why the voice was familiar: it was Sadie's boyfriend, Clay! I felt anger rising up inside of me. How could he be so callous? Sadie would be mortified to know he was showing her bull-riding wreck to other people! And how did he happen to have a video of the wreck? He must have been the one who was running the controls on the bull!

My train of thought derailed as I heard the second voice ask, "How come you haven't shared this?"

"We got an agreement that if one of the guys on our team gets dumped in practice, no one can post a video online."

"Well, *she's* not on your team, is she?"

"No," said Clay. "Guess that means…" There was a brief silence. "Okay. Shared."

"Cool."

I couldn't help myself. I stepped around the corner. "Clay Corson, how can you do that to Sadie?"

The three boys looked up in surprise.

Clay stammered in response: "Wha— What do you mean? Do what?"

"Where should I start?" I asked angrily. "First of all, why did she even get on that bull? She never wanted to ride it. You must've talked her into it."

"Don't go blaming me," he said. "It's your fault she got on it. She saw you two do it and figured she could do it easy. I told her not to, but she made up her mind."

"I don't believe you," I said. "Sadie has never cared about riding the bull. All she ever wanted to do was watch you guys riding it."

He swelled up with pride. "Yeah. She definitely thinks us bull riders are cool."

"Except you're not actually a bull rider, Clay," I said. "You're a bull faller."

He looked angry at that.

I didn't care, but just plowed ahead. "In all the time I've watched you guys practicing, I don't think I've ever seen you manage to ride that thing. In fact, I think I've ridden it more times than you have, and that's been a grand total of once!"

His two 'friends' snorted with suppressed laughter, which seemed to deflate him a little.

I probably should have turned away, but I wanted answers. "And how could you post a video of her getting dumped and hurt like that, just for your friends' entertainment?"

"Nah, it's not like that," he claimed. "People are gonna see this video and see how gutsy she is. Yeah… gutsy. And hot!"

"Seriously? That's what you expect people to see? It didn't sound as if that's what your buddies here were seeing. They were all about watching her getting 'launched' and 'catching some air.'"

"Aw, c'mon. It's a great wreck," he said. "And she didn't get hurt."

Chapter 13 - The Dance

"Are you kidding me?" I demanded. "They kept her in the hospital overnight because they were worried about a brain injury. That's serious!"

"Maybe for some wussy rider like you, it is," he sneered, "but Sadie's not like you."

Autumn Rose broke in. "Why didn't you stay to help Sadie after she fell off, Clay?"

"She was fine!" he said. "She just wanted to sit there and see the video. She didn't want any help."

"I can't believe what a lying, sorry piece of trash you are!" I blurted out.

Clay's look turned from surprise to anger and he stepped toward me, fists clenched. But, just as quickly, his face changed again and he slunk backward a step.

I'd had a moment of panic when he'd started in my direction. Then, when he sorta deflated and stepped back, I wasn't sure what to think. Until I heard the voice behind me.

"That's a whole lot nicer term than I would've used, Meghan." It was Lane's voice. Then to Clay, he said, "Do I understand correctly that you just posted a video of my little sister coming off that mechanical bull? Because if you did, you better hope you can delete it before anyone else sees it." His voice was very low, very quiet, and dripping with anger.

"Aw, c'mon, man," Clay said, some of his usual bravado coming back into his voice and his posture. "It's no big deal. People will get to see how gutsy Sadie is. And how great-looking! She'll think it's cool!"

"No, I won't," Sadie said, as she stepped around the corner behind her brother. "You told me not to tell anyone that you talked me into getting on that bull. I lied to my own brother for you, Clay."

"How stupid are you?" Lane interrupted. (I thought for a second he was talking to Sadie, but then realized it was Clay's stupidity he was calling out.) "You just posted the proof that you were the one who was with her."

Sadie continued angrily, "You knew I didn't want to ride that bull, Clay, but you just kept telling me I should."

"Sadie…" Clay started.

"And now I find out you posted that video, making me look like a fool!" she said, sounding hurt.

Before Clay could answer, Lane stepped forward. "I wanna know why you left my sister when you knew she was hurt!" he demanded. "Why didn't you call for help? She was sitting in the lean-to, holding her head, when I found her, and you were nowhere!"

"Yeah well, Sadie an' me didn't want anyone to know she'd had help with the bull. That's all. We wanted everyone to figure she was just brave all by herself." He flashed a smile at Sadie.

She wasn't having it. "You know that's a lie, Clay. You were scared you'd get kicked off the team. You asked me to lie to protect you. And I did." Sadie burst into tears and said once again, "I lied to my own brother."

Chapter 13 - The Dance

Turning on Clay, Lane continued, "And *you*, you coward, you videoed her, then left when she got hurt, so no one would know you'd been the one who started the whole mess! I oughta—" Lane said as he stepped toward Clay, fists clenched.

Sadie lunged for her brother, grabbing an arm. "Please don't, Lane! He's not worth it. I know you can flatten him in a fight, but you'll get kicked off the rodeo team, so don't! Just don't! I'm finally eligible for the team this year, and I've been looking forward to rodeoing with you for the past two years. Please! Just walk away!"

Lane's forward momentum faltered and he allowed his little sister to turn him back toward the door, though not before telling Clay, "You take that video down. And don't you get anywhere near my sister again!"

Sadie turned to her brother. "Lane, who I see is *my* decision, not yours."

Clay smirked at Lane.

Turning back to Clay, Sadie continued, "And I will tell you for a fact, Clay Corson, I never want to see you again."

Clay's mouth dropped open in surprise. "But—"

"I don't want you ever talking to me again. I mean, I know I'll have to put up with seeing you around school and at rodeos, and even at our place when you come for bull practice. But Clay, you just treat me like a total stranger," she said. "One who clearly sees the white stripe down your back and *knows* you're nothing but a skunk."

Sadie still had a hand on her brother's arm. She grabbed my wrist with her other hand and pulled me along with her brother, back around the corner and into the dance. Autumn Rose was in front of us and sorta got swept along too.

As soon as we were inside the building, Sadie released my arm and said, "I need to go fix my makeup." As she let go of her brother, she demanded, "Don't you go back out there!"

"I won't," he said.

"Promise me!"

Lane grinned down at her. "I promise."

Sadie started to walk away, but Lane's voice stopped her. "I'm proud of you, baby sister."

She flashed a smile his direction, then continued on her mission.

Autumn Rose and I followed Sadie into the ladies' room where she started using cold, damp paper towels, trying to chase away the blotchy redness on her face that gave away the fact that she'd been half crying and all angry.

"I'm sorry I lied to you both when you came to see me." She looked from Autumn Rose to me and then back to Autumn Rose. "I could tell you both saw through it, but I felt I had to lie to protect Clay." The way she said Clay's name, it sounded as if she was trying to spit his name out.

Chapter 13 - The Dance

Autumn Rose's expression didn't change, and she didn't say anything; she just waited for Sadie to explain. By the time Sadie had finished, Autumn Rose still hadn't said a word. Finally, after a full fifteen seconds of silence, which felt like about fifteen minutes, Autumn Rose said, "Your word is important, Sadie. I'm glad, for your sake, you're starting to figure that out. I accept your apology."

"I do too," I said.

"Thank you," she said. "Your friendship is important to me. I've really missed you both."

"Now, we better get out there before my parents come looking for us," Autumn Rose said. "And unless you want to tell your story to them, we need to act normal."

"Normal?" I asked. "I've never been to a dance before. I don't know what 'normal' is."

"It's talking, dancing, and having fun!" Sadie said, with her usual sparkle returning. She turned and started out the door. Looking back over her shoulder, she said, "Normally, I'd be saying things like Wow! Meghan, you look really nice tonight."

I felt myself blushing a little, happy for the compliment.

Almost immediately she got that ornery look in her eyes and said, "I thought you only ever put make-up on for horse shows," then laughed, and disappeared into the crowd. A lot more people had shown up while we'd been talking, and the dance floor was pretty crowded.

"Do you dance as well as you ride bulls?"

I turned around, surprised to see Lane.

"Probably not," I giggled nervously, "but let's find out."

We danced a fast dance. I felt awkward, all arms and legs that I didn't quite know what to do with. When that song ended, Lane walked me over to the table where Autumn Rose had returned to sit with her folks. "Coach Ifaita, may I dance with your daughter?"

"You have my permission. But you'd better ask her," he responded.

Lane held his hand out to Autumn Rose, who took it and stood up. As they walked onto the dance floor, I sat down in Autumn Rose's chair. But soon, another member of the rodeo team walked up and asked me to dance. That's how it went. I sat for a song or two, then danced for a song. When I wasn't dancing, I watched carefully, trying to figure out what I was supposed to be doing. My confidence started to grow a little and, with it, my movements got a little bigger, which turned out not to be a good plan. The soles of my cowboy boots were slick and down I went, landing on my backside on the dance floor.

My dance partner reached down and helped me up, while another cowboy shouted, "The horses and the bulls can't put this girl on the ground, but this floor sure got it done."

Everyone laughed, including me. I think my laugh was to hide my embarrassment, since I know for a fact that I didn't think it was funny. But at least the soreness went away quickly, and I wasn't going to have to quit riding, like Jeannie had. She'd have been furious.

I went back over to sit down, but another guy came up and said, "You gotta climb back on after you get bucked off, so c'mon. Show that dance floor who's boss."

I went out there and kinda reverted to feeling awkward and unsure of myself. But at least I stayed on my feet. And I had fun!

After the last dance ended, Autumn Rose and Lane walked back over to the table. "Good night, Coach. Good night, Mrs. Ifaita." Then he turned to Autumn Rose. "I'll see you Monday at Jeannie's. I've got my first English lesson at ten o'clock."

⸻

At the barn the next morning, Threepio followed me around while I did my chores. Once I was done, I scooped him up into my arms. "You are such a sweet boy, Threep," I told him as he settled against me, purring. "You showed up here last spring, not knowing how much your life would change by being here. But look at you now! You're sleek and handsome and happy."

I continued petting Threepio while I watched Freckles licking the last few morsels of grain out of his feed tub. "And you, Freckles. You've turned into an English horse along with being my super cow horse and reining horse. And you're clearly having fun with all of it!"

Change. Both of them had changed.

Maybe I was changing too.

"Know what?" I asked my two four-legged friends, "I think maybe it's okay to learn new things and try new things. Even going to a dance. Embarrassing as falling was, it didn't actually ruin anything. The world didn't stop spinning. In fact, except for the fall, it was kinda fun."

Threepio stretched out a front leg, touching my nose gently with his paw and causing me to giggle.

"But there's nothing more fun than cuddling a goofy cat," I told him. Then, as Freckles reached over the fence and nuzzled my cheek, I added, "unless it's having a great horse."

About the Author

My stories are largely based on my own and/or my riding students' experiences.

Throughout my entire life I've been blessed to learn from top horsemen and horsewomen in various fields, including reining, jumping, colt-starting, three-day eventing, and timed events. There are some things that seem to be common across all the disciplines:

- The more you learn, the more you will realize you need to learn.

- The goal is to develop your horse into your partner. Listen to him/her and always communicate in a way that the horse can understand. A scared or upset horse (or student) cannot learn.

- Individuals learn differently, and if the method you're using is upsetting your horse or student, it's on you to figure out a way to make things clear to them.

- Along with fair, clear communication, there must also be time for the horse and student to think and understand.

Learning is, indeed, a lifelong commitment, and I continue to learn as I continue to teach and to write.

↬ When some bull riders started ragging my husband (actually, fiancé in those days) and me about our "sissy English saddles," we stepped off our horses, walked over to their mechanical bucking bull, then rode it, each of us for the full eight seconds. The guys were a good deal more respectful after that.

Printed in the USA
CPSIA information can be obtained
at www.ICGtesting.com
JSHW052201100923
47985JS00005B/19